5일 완성 토익스피킹 멀티템플릿 실전북

초판 1판 2쇄 발행 2024. 02. 01
저자 정하진
펴낸곳 (주)티처케이
출판 총괄 이예빈
편집 총괄 이수진
디자인 심혜영
홈페이지 https://www.teacherk.kr
주소 서울특별시 강남구 테헤란로 6길 33 와이엔케이빌딩 2층

도서문의 안내
전화 070-8856-0487
팩스 0504-842-0487
이메일 teacherk@teacherk.kr

5일 완성

토익스피킹
멀티템플릿
실전북

CONTENTS :

토익스피킹 정보

1 시험의 목적과 특징

업무환경에서 영어 말하기 능력을 평가하는 시험입니다. 미국 ETS에서 개발하고 한국 토익위원회가 주관하는 국제공인 시험이며, 인터넷을 이용하여 컴퓨터로 보는 IBT (Internet - Based Test) 방식의 시험입니다. 시험 응시 중 필기가 가능하며, 시험장에서 배부된 용지와 필기구만 사용 가능합니다.

2 시험시간, 응시 빈도

시험 시간은 약 13-15분 정도이며, 총 11개의 문항으로 평가합니다.
시험 전 오리엔테이션이 진행되며, 시험 후 본인의 답변을 확인하는 시간이 주어집니다.

시험은 하루에 최대 1회 응시할 수 있으며, 주 단위 응시횟수 제약은 없습니다.
주로 토요일, 일요일에 시험이 열리지만, 간혹 무작위로 평일에 열리기도 합니다.
시간대는 오전, 오후 다양하지만 주말 오전 시간대가 주를 이룹니다.

3 시험의 구성

문항 번호	문제 유형	준비 시간	답변 시간	평가 기준	점수
1 - 2	지문 읽기	각 45초	각 45초	발음, 억양, 강세	3점
3 - 4	사진 묘사하기	각 45초	각 30초	(위 항목 포함) 문법, 어휘, 일관성	3점
5 - 7	질문에 답하기	각 3초	15 / 15 / 30초	(위 항목 포함) 내용 관련성, 완성도	3점
8 - 10	제공된 정보를 사용해 질문에 답하기	표 읽기 45초 각 3초	15 / 15 / 30초	위의 모든 항목	3점
11	의견 말하기	45초	60초	위의 모든 항목	5점

* 문항별 준비시간과 답변 시간은 상이합니다.
* 점수는 200점 만점으로 환산되어 표기됩니다.
* 10번의 경우 질문이 2회 안내됩니다.

4 점수별 등급

등급	점수
Advanced High	200
Advanced Mid	180 ~ 190
Advanced Low	160 ~ 170
Intermediate High	140 ~ 150
Intermediate Mid 3	130
Intermediate Mid 2	120
Intermediate Mid 1	110
Intermediate Low	90 ~ 100
Novice High	60 ~ 80
Novice Mid / Low	0 ~ 50

5 토익스피킹 시험 채점 방식

응시자 답변

IBT 시스템
응시자의
답변 녹음파일
ETS 본사로
전송됨

ETS 채점
채점 당일
Calibration Test를
통과한 채점관이
답변 채점

환산 과정
환산 과정을 거쳐
최종 성적 산출

성적 발표

* Calibration Test란?
정확한 평가를 위해 ETS 전문 rater(채점관)가 채점 당일 날 반드시 통과해야 하는 시험이며, 시험 개발자들이 채점한 답변들을 다시 채점하는 시험입니다. 시험 개발자와 일정수준 동일한 채점을 해야만 채점관으로 참여할 수 있습니다.

실전북 특장점

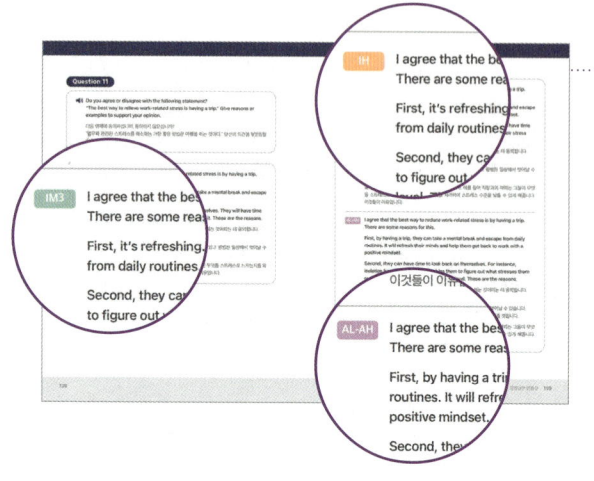

등급별 답변 템플릿 제공

7, 11번의 IM, IH, AL+ 등급별 모범 답변 제공으로 목표 점수에 따라 필요한 부분만 집중해서 학습할 수 있습니다.

정확한 등급별 득점 포인트 제시

[발음, 억양, 강세, 문법, 어휘, 일관성, 답변 완성도]
파트별 채점 기준을 완벽하게 분석하여 정체된 점수를 빠르게 높일 수 있는 핵심포인트를 명쾌하게 제공합니다.

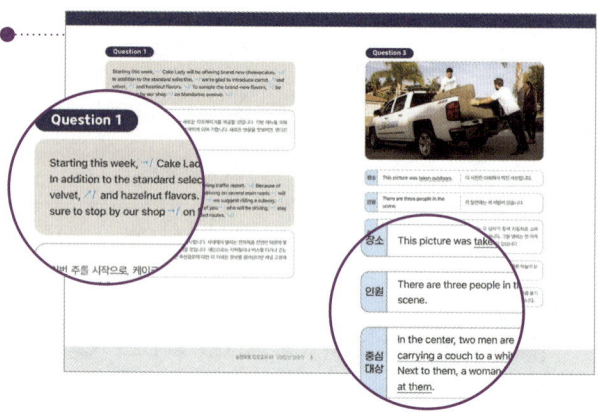

출제 확률이 높은 실전문제 엄선

최신유형을 완벽하게 분석한 모의고사가 20회분 수록되어 실전감각을 극대화 시킬 수 있습니다.

모의고사 동영상 제공

실전유형 모의고사로 개별실력 점검 및 파악

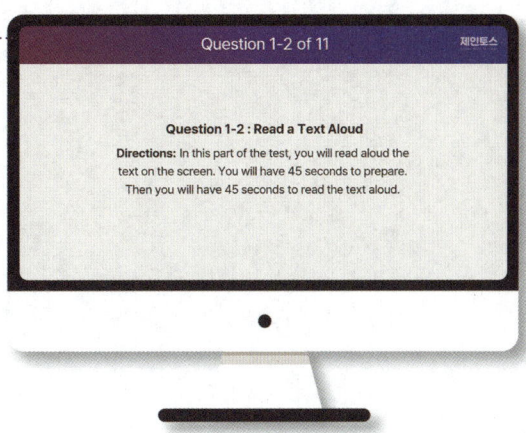

실전유형 온라인 모의고사

(PDF) - 추가 5회분

템플릿 요약본 (PDF)

음원 다운로드

핵심내용이 수록된 자료로
언제 어디서나 효율성 높은 학습 가능

모범답변 해설강의

해설강의 문제풀이를 통해
제인쌤의 노하우 전수

01

실전유형
모의고사

Question 1-2 : Read a Text Aloud

Directions: In this part of the test, you will read aloud the text on the screen. You will have 45 seconds to prepare. Then you will have 45 seconds to read the text aloud.

Question 1 of 11

Starting this week, Cake Lady will be offering brand new cheesecakes. In addition to the standard selection, we're glad to introduce carrot, red velvet, and hazelnut flavors. To sample the brand-new flavors, be sure to stop by our shop on Mandarine avenue.

PREPARATION TIME	RESPONSE TIME
00:00:45	00:00:45

Question 2 of 11

Thanks for tuning in to Kingsville's morning traffic report. Because of the electronics convention downtown, driving on several main roads will be slower than usual. For alternatives, we suggest riding a subway, taking a bus, or walking. For those of you who will be driving, stay tuned for more details on recommended routes.

PREPARATION TIME	RESPONSE TIME
00:00:45	00:00:45

Question 3-4 : Describe a Picture

Directions: In this part of the test, you will describe the picture on your screen in as much detail as you can. You will have 45 seconds to prepare your response. Then you will have 30 seconds to speak about the picture.

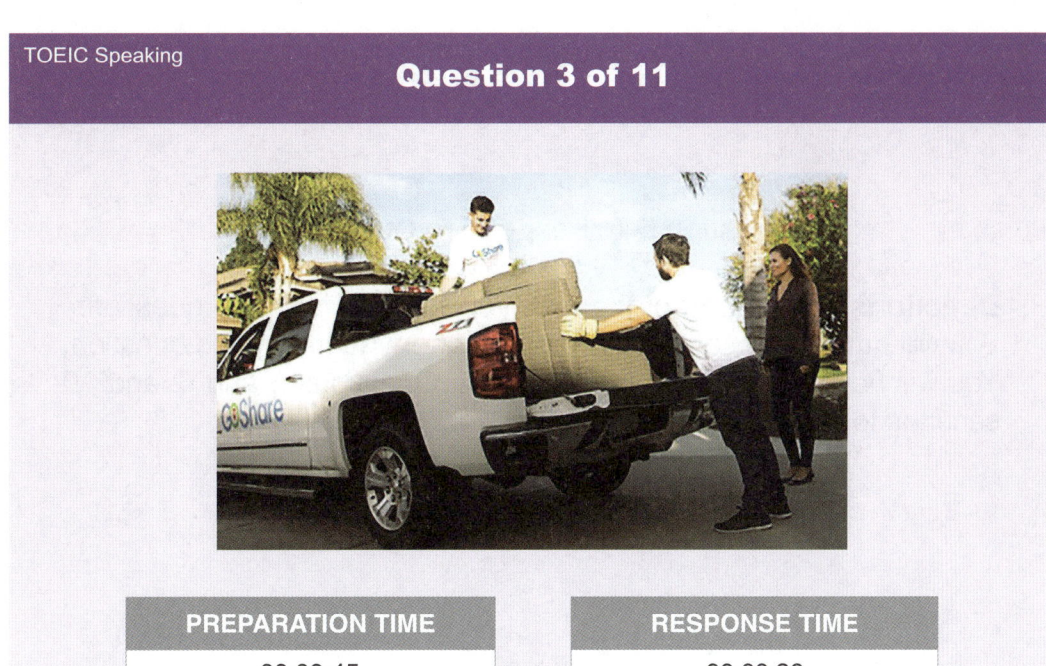

PREPARATION TIME	RESPONSE TIME
00:00:45	00:00:30

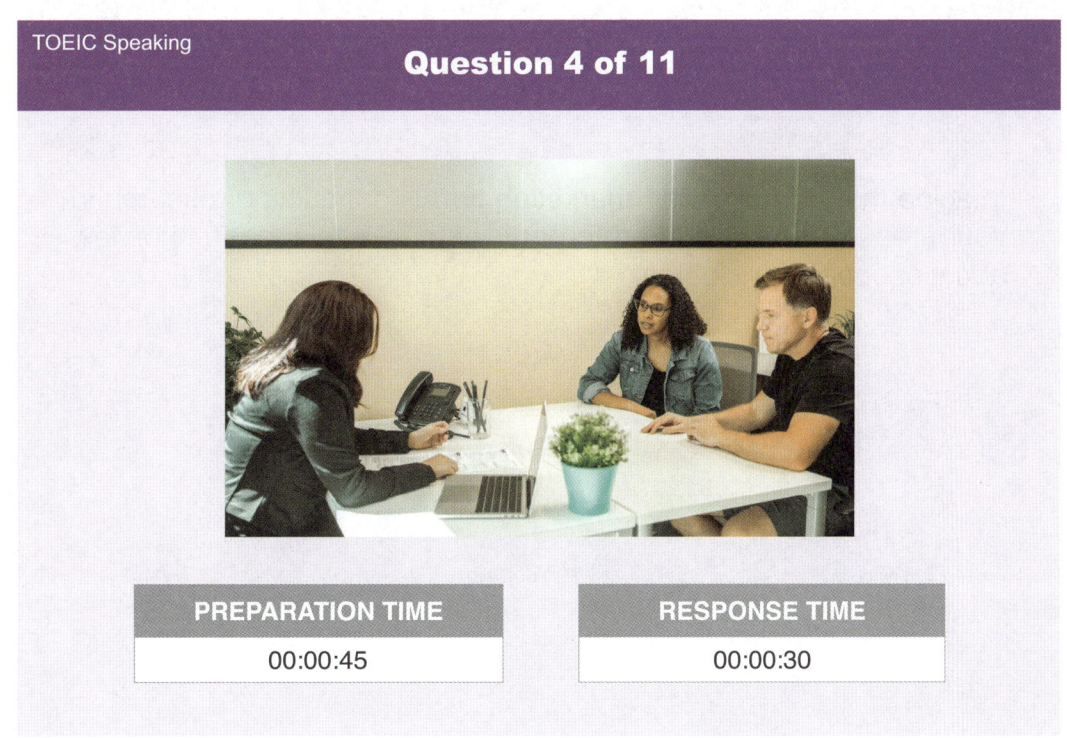

PREPARATION TIME	RESPONSE TIME
00:00:45	00:00:30

Question 5-7 : Respond to Questions

Directions: In this part of the test, you will answer three questions. You will have three seconds to prepare after you hear each question. You will have 15 seconds to respond to Questions 5 and 6, and 30 seconds to respond to Question 7.

Imagine that an Australian marketing firm is conducting research in your area. You have agreed to participate in a telephone interview about shopping for clothes.

Question 5 of 11

When was the last time you shopped for clothes, and what did you buy?

PREPARATION TIME	RESPONSE TIME
00:00:03	00:00:15

Question 6 of 11

Besides price, what is the most important consideration for you when deciding which clothes to buy, and why?

PREPARATION TIME	RESPONSE TIME
00:00:03	00:00:15

Question 7 of 11

If you were going to buy athletic wear, would you rather go to a sporting goods store or a regular clothing store, and why?

PREPARATION TIME	RESPONSE TIME
00:00:03	00:00:30

Question 8-10 : Respond to Questions Using Information Provided

Directions: In this part of the test, you will answer three questions based on the information provided. You will have 45 seconds to read the information before the questions begin. You will have three seconds to prepare and 15 seconds to respond to Questions 8 and 9. You will hear Question 10 two times. You will have three seconds to prepare and 30 seconds to respond to Question 10.

Question 8-10 of 11

Orange corporation
Marketing team manager, Jim Parker / Itinerary for business trip

Depart Beijing, Vase airlines, flight 127 Arrive Seoul	2:15 P.M. 4:00 P.M.	April 16 April 16
Depart Seoul, Vase airlines, flight 516 Arrive Beijing (lunch provided in the flight)	1:50 P.M. 3:05 P.M.	April 21 April 21
[Accommodation] Central view hotel, room 203 (non-smoking)	Check-in 2:00 P.M. Check-out 11:00 A.M.	April 16-21
[Car rental] Car delivered to Central view hotel Return to the Mobeez rental office	4:00 P.M. 5:00 P.M.	April 16 April 21

PREPARATION TIME
00:00:45

Q8

PREPARATION TIME	RESPONSE TIME
00:00:03	00:00:15

Q9

PREPARATION TIME	RESPONSE TIME
00:00:03	00:00:15

Q10

PREPARATION TIME	RESPONSE TIME
00:00:03	00:00:30

Question 11 : Express an Opinion

Directions: In this part of the test, you will give your opinion about a specific topic. Be sure to say as much as you can in the time allowed. You will have 45 seconds to prepare. Then you will have 60 seconds to speak.

Do you agree or disagree with the following statement?
"The best way to relieve work-related stress is having a trip."
Give reasons or examples to support your opinion.

PREPARATION TIME	RESPONSE TIME
00:00:45	00:00:60

MEMO

02

실전유형
모의고사

Question 1-2 : Read a Text Aloud

Directions: In this part of the test, you will read aloud the text on the screen. You will have 45 seconds to prepare. Then you will have 45 seconds to read the text aloud.

TOEIC Speaking

Question 1 of 11

Thank you for calling Mandio's, the most popular restaurant in the city. We will be with you shortly to take your order for your favorite burger, sandwich, or salad. For faster services, you can order online on our website. Also, our website provides specific details about our special items.

PREPARATION TIME	RESPONSE TIME
00:00:45	00:00:45

TOEIC Speaking

Question 2 of 11

You are listening to Radio Seven's entertainment and media report. Our first guest in this morning is Simon Clark, the producer of the Oscar-winning documentary film Night Mail. On today's show, Mr. Clark will tell us about his background, experiences in film making and his other projects. Now, let's welcome Mr. Clark.

PREPARATION TIME	RESPONSE TIME
00:00:45	00:00:45

Question 3-4 : Describe a Picture

Directions: In this part of the test, you will describe the picture on your screen in as much detail as you can. You will have 45 seconds to prepare your response. Then you will have 30 seconds to speak about the picture.

PREPARATION TIME	RESPONSE TIME
00:00:45	00:00:30

PREPARATION TIME	RESPONSE TIME
00:00:45	00:00:30

Question 5-7 : Respond to Questions

Directions: In this part of the test, you will answer three questions. You will have three seconds to prepare after you hear each question. You will have 15 seconds to respond to Questions 5 and 6, and 30 seconds to respond to Question 7.

Imagine that the US marketing firm is conducting research about streaming services that you use to watch television shows.
A streaming service is a service that sends videos or music over the internet so that people can watch or listen to it immediately rather than having to download it.

Question 5 of 11

How often do you stream television shows and what do you usually watch?

PREPARATION TIME	RESPONSE TIME
00:00:03	00:00:15

Question 6 of 11

When was the last time you streamed a television show and what service did you use?

PREPARATION TIME	RESPONSE TIME
00:00:03	00:00:15

Question 7 of 11

When deciding which streaming service to use, which is a more influential factor in your decision-making: other viewers' reviews on the service or advertisements of the service?

PREPARATION TIME	RESPONSE TIME
00:00:03	00:00:30

Question 8-10 : Respond to Questions Using Information Provided

Directions: In this part of the test, you will answer three questions based on the information provided. You will have 45 seconds to read the information before the questions begin. You will have three seconds to prepare and 15 seconds to respond to Questions 8 and 9. You will hear Question 10 two times. You will have three seconds to prepare and 30 seconds to respond to Question 10.

Business Seminar for Small Businesses

[Global E-business Association] May 15, Wednesday, Leonardo Hall 203

9:00 A.M. - 10:00 A.M.	Welcome address	Jennifer Miller
10:00 A.M. - 11:00 A.M.	Introducing new approaches of market analysis	Lisa Henderson
11:00 A.M. - 12:00 P.M.	Lunch	-
12:00 P.M. - 1:00 P.M.	Lecture: time management and using resources	Wayne Xia
1:00 P.M. - 2:00 P.M.	Workshop: improving marketing strategies	Alan Callie
2:00 P.M. - 3:00 P.M.	Discussion: 5 steps of online market research (computer-based, laptops required)	Lisa Henderson
3:00 P.M. - 4:00 P.M.	Lecture: ways to think differently	Sue Chang

PREPARATION TIME
00:00:45

Q8

PREPARATION TIME	RESPONSE TIME
00:00:03	00:00:15

Q9

PREPARATION TIME	RESPONSE TIME
00:00:03	00:00:15

Q10

PREPARATION TIME	RESPONSE TIME
00:00:03	00:00:30

Question 11 : Express an Opinion

Directions: In this part of the test, you will give your opinion about a specific topic. Be sure to say as much as you can in the time allowed. You will have 45 seconds to prepare. Then you will have 60 seconds to speak.

Which of the following would contribute the MOST to living a satisfying life? Give causes or examples to support your opinion.

- Having a nice job
- Exercising regularly
- Spending time with loved ones

PREPARATION TIME	RESPONSE TIME
00:00:45	00:00:60

MEMO

03

실전유형
모의고사

Question 1-2 : Read a Text Aloud

Directions: In this part of the test, you will read aloud the text on the screen. You will have 45 seconds to prepare. Then you will have 45 seconds to read the text aloud.

Question 1 of 11

Hello and welcome to Everson music podcast. Today, I am joined by Gabriel Fletcher, an assistant professor at Central University. We'll be discussing some of the greatest albums of the past year. We'll start by reviewing my favorite pop, classical, and jazz artists.

PREPARATION TIME	RESPONSE TIME
00:00:45	00:00:45

Question 2 of 11

Thank you for volunteering today at our Art museum's Family Day. You are going to be supporting our staff in a variety of ways. To begin, please report to the reception desk. You will get your information form, your museum badge, and a voucher for the cafeteria. If you need help finding anything, please ask one of our staffs.

PREPARATION TIME	RESPONSE TIME
00:00:45	00:00:45

Question 3-4 : Describe a Picture

Directions: In this part of the test, you will describe the picture on your screen in as much detail as you can. You will have 45 seconds to prepare your response. Then you will have 30 seconds to speak about the picture.

PREPARATION TIME	RESPONSE TIME
00:00:45	00:00:30

PREPARATION TIME	RESPONSE TIME
00:00:45	00:00:30

Question 5-7 : Respond to Questions

Directions: In this part of the test, you will answer three questions. You will have three seconds to prepare after you hear each question. You will have 15 seconds to respond to Questions 5 and 6, and 30 seconds to respond to Question 7.

Imagine that World Vision Company is conducting research in your area. You have agreed to participate in a telephone interview about donating money for organizations.

Question 5 of 11

Do you think it is a good idea for charities or organizations to ask people to donate money on the radio? Why or why not?

PREPARATION TIME		RESPONSE TIME
00:00:03		00:00:15

Question 6 of 11

Do you ever use a mobile phone to donate your money? Why or why not?

PREPARATION TIME		RESPONSE TIME
00:00:03		00:00:15

Question 7 of 11

Which of the following organizations would you be willing to donate to, and why?

- An environmental organization
- An organization that does medical research
- An educational organization

PREPARATION TIME		RESPONSE TIME
00:00:03		00:00:30

Question 8-10 : Respond to Questions Using Information Provided

Directions: In this part of the test, you will answer three questions based on the information provided. You will have 45 seconds to read the information before the questions begin. You will have three seconds to prepare and 15 seconds to respond to Questions 8 and 9. You will hear Question 10 two times. You will have three seconds to prepare and 30 seconds to respond to Question 10.

Question 8-10 of 11

Schedule on February 4
Richard McDonald Executive director, Interesting Corporation

9:00 - 11:00 A.M.	Conference call (CEO, Dellie food)
11:00 A.M. - Noon	Meeting (Donald Fella, manager, financial department)
Noon - 1:00 P.M.	Presentation (new employees, R&R)
1:00 - 2:00 P.M.	~~Lunch with Marta Jones~~ *moved to March 5, 4 P.M.*
2:00 - 3:00 P.M.	Online communication with Applicants
3:00 - 4:00 P.M.	Meeting (Marie Darren, manager, marketing department)
4:00 - 5:00 P.M.	Review, sales performance (director, sales department)

PREPARATION TIME
00:00:45

Q8

PREPARATION TIME	RESPONSE TIME
00:00:03	00:00:15

Q9

PREPARATION TIME	RESPONSE TIME
00:00:03	00:00:15

Q10

PREPARATION TIME	RESPONSE TIME
00:00:03	00:00:30

Question 11 : Express an Opinion

Directions: In this part of the test, you will give your opinion about a specific topic. Be sure to say as much as you can in the time allowed. You will have 45 seconds to prepare. Then you will have 60 seconds to speak.

Do you agree or disagree with the following statement?
"A person's job satisfaction is affected more by salary than the assigned duties."

PREPARATION TIME	RESPONSE TIME
00:00:45	00:00:60

MEMO

04

실전유형
모의고사

Question 1-2 : Read a Text Aloud

Directions: In this part of the test, you will read aloud the text on the screen. You will have 45 seconds to prepare. Then you will have 45 seconds to read the text aloud.

Question 1 of 11

If you are not getting the cell phone service you want, consider switching to Johnson mobile. Our service is faster, more reliable, and more affordable than anything you'll find on the market. And we are providing a free service for three weeks to new customers. So, call us now.

PREPARATION TIME	RESPONSE TIME
00:00:45	00:00:45

Question 2 of 11

Hello, and welcome to the seminar on social media for business. This seminar is to help you enhance marketing strategies of your business sales, brand awareness and customer loyalty. Social media, a powerful marketing tool, can help you achieve these goals. As a first step, we will provide you essential tips and advice to use popular apps in an effective way to make customers interested in your services.

PREPARATION TIME	RESPONSE TIME
00:00:45	00:00:45

Question 3-4 : Describe a Picture

Directions: In this part of the test, you will describe the picture on your screen in as much detail as you can. You will have 45 seconds to prepare your response. Then you will have 30 seconds to speak about the picture.

PREPARATION TIME	RESPONSE TIME
00:00:45	00:00:30

PREPARATION TIME	RESPONSE TIME
00:00:45	00:00:30

Question 5-7 : Respond to Questions

Directions: In this part of the test, you will answer three questions. You will have three seconds to prepare after you hear each question. You will have 15 seconds to respond to Questions 5 and 6, and 30 seconds to respond to Question 7.

Imagine a marketing firm is conducting research in your community. You have agreed to participate in a telephone interview about birthday gifts.

Question 5 of 11

When was the last time you gave a birthday gift, and who was it for?

PREPARATION TIME	RESPONSE TIME
00:00:03	00:00:15

Question 6 of 11

Which makes a better birthday gift: money or a present from a store, and why?

PREPARATION TIME	RESPONSE TIME
00:00:03	00:00:15

Question 7 of 11

Many couples these days make a list of birthday gifts that they want to receive and exchange it with each other. Do you think it is a good idea for them to do this? Why or why not?

PREPARATION TIME	RESPONSE TIME
00:00:03	00:00:30

Question 8-10 : Respond to Questions Using Information Provided

Directions: In this part of the test, you will answer three questions based on the information provided. You will have 45 seconds to read the information before the questions begin. You will have three seconds to prepare and 15 seconds to respond to Questions 8 and 9. You will hear Question 10 two times. You will have three seconds to prepare and 30 seconds to respond to Question 10.

Conference of food scientists
Rayon hotel, Tony ballroom

September 21, Thursday	9:00 - 10:00 A.M.	Registration (hotel lobby)
	10:00 - 11:00 A.M.	Presentation: boosting nutrition through food science (Jack Nicole)
	11:00 A.M. - Noon	Workshop: updates on global food standards (Lora Kimberly)
	Noon - 1:00 P.M.	Discussion: meals for children under 9
September 22, Friday	9:00 - 10:00 A.M.	Breakfast (Tillet dining hall)
	10:00 - 11:00 A.M.	Workshop: a closer look at food preservation (Jason Molina)
	11:00 A.M. - Noon	Lecture: how to choose the right ingredients for the elderly (Bobby Lim)
	Noon - 1:00 P.M.	Closing remarks

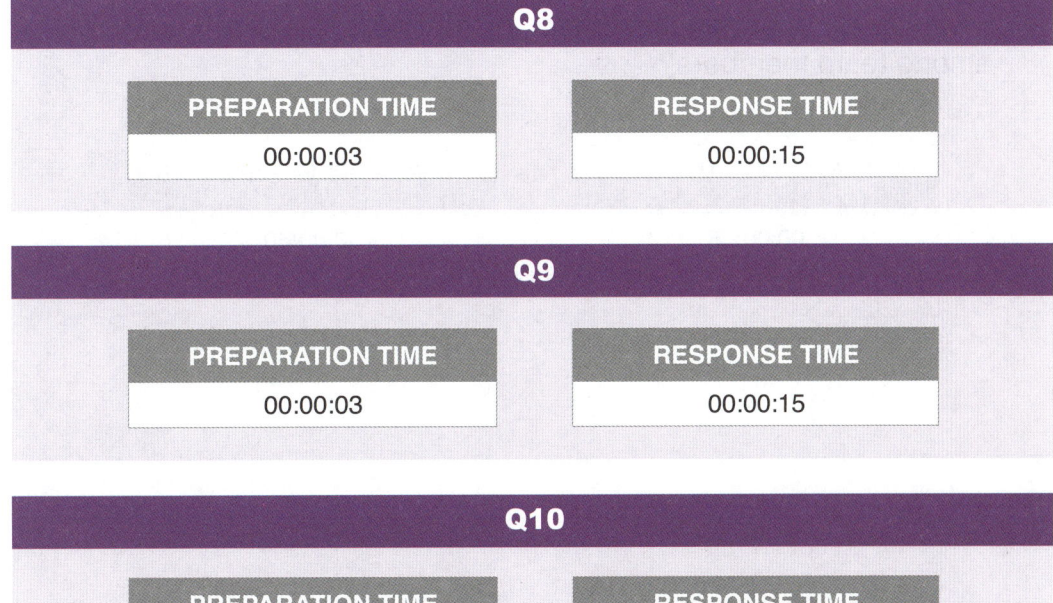

PREPARATION TIME
00:00:45

Q8

PREPARATION TIME	RESPONSE TIME
00:00:03	00:00:15

Q9

PREPARATION TIME	RESPONSE TIME
00:00:03	00:00:15

Q10

PREPARATION TIME	RESPONSE TIME
00:00:03	00:00:30

Question 11 : Express an Opinion

Directions: In this part of the test, you will give your opinion about a specific topic. Be sure to say as much as you can in the time allowed. You will have 45 seconds to prepare. Then you will have 60 seconds to speak.

Which do you think contributes more to a team's effectiveness : having an experienced leader or having a good relationship among team members?

PREPARATION TIME	RESPONSE TIME
00:00:45	00:00:60

MEMO

05

실전유형
모의고사

Question 1-2 : Read a Text Aloud

Directions: In this part of the test, you will read aloud the text on the screen. You will have 45 seconds to prepare. Then you will have 45 seconds to read the text aloud.

Question 1 of 11

Good morning, College Radio listeners. In weather forecast, today is supposed to be a beautiful sunny day. It's a great day to study outdoors, go to a coffee shop, or walk in the park. We anticipate a moderate breeze, which will make pleasant winds while in the sunshine.

PREPARATION TIME	RESPONSE TIME
00:00:45	00:00:45

Question 2 of 11

Thank you for inviting me to speak at this month's Medical Care Conference. Before I begin my speech, let me provide a brief interview. In the past year, I conducted hundreds of interviews with doctors, patients and other hospital staffs. I will be sharing a few things I noticed about how hospitals can provide the best medical treatment to their patients.

PREPARATION TIME	RESPONSE TIME
00:00:45	00:00:45

Question 3-4 : Describe a Picture

Directions: In this part of the test, you will describe the picture on your screen in as much detail as you can. You will have 45 seconds to prepare your response. Then you will have 30 seconds to speak about the picture.

PREPARATION TIME	RESPONSE TIME
00:00:45	00:00:30

PREPARATION TIME	RESPONSE TIME
00:00:45	00:00:30

Question 5-7 : Respond to Questions

Directions: In this part of the test, you will answer three questions. You will have three seconds to prepare after you hear each question. You will have 15 seconds to respond to Questions 5 and 6, and 30 seconds to respond to Question 7.

Imagine a newspaper company is conducting research in your area about listening to an audio podcast. A podcast is an episodic series of digital audio files that a user can download to a personal device to listen. You have agreed to participate in a telephone interview about your listening habits.

Question 5 of 11

When was the last time you listened to an audio podcast, and what was it about?

PREPARATION TIME	RESPONSE TIME
00:00:03	00:00:15

Question 6 of 11

Would you listen to a podcast when taking a train or bus? Why or why not?

PREPARATION TIME	RESPONSE TIME
00:00:03	00:00:15

Question 7 of 11

What are the advantages of listening to an audio podcast instead of reading a book?

PREPARATION TIME	RESPONSE TIME
00:00:03	00:00:30

Question 8-10 : Respond to Questions Using Information Provided

Directions: In this part of the test, you will answer three questions based on the information provided. You will have 45 seconds to read the information before the questions begin. You will have three seconds to prepare and 15 seconds to respond to Questions 8 and 9. You will hear Question 10 two times. You will have three seconds to prepare and 30 seconds to respond to Question 10.

LulkerBe Nature Park Running Trail
Open daily, May through November, 9 A.M. – 7 P.M.

Trail	Challenge	Distance	Note
Nathan peak	Difficult	10 kilometers	Stiff hills
Lone trail	Difficult	8 kilometers	
Wilson road	Difficult	9 kilometers	Cross bike trail
Tomato trail	Easy	2 kilometers	
Breeze rail	Intermediate	4 kilometers	
Wecantte Neva	Easy	1 kilometer	Designed for beginners
Ages 15 or younger should be accompanied by an adult			

PREPARATION TIME
00:00:45

Q8

PREPARATION TIME	RESPONSE TIME
00:00:03	00:00:15

Q9

PREPARATION TIME	RESPONSE TIME
00:00:03	00:00:15

Q10

PREPARATION TIME	RESPONSE TIME
00:00:03	00:00:30

Question 11 : Express an Opinion

Directions: In this part of the test, you will give your opinion about a specific topic. Be sure to say as much as you can in the time allowed. You will have 45 seconds to prepare. Then you will have 60 seconds to speak.

Do you agree or disagree with the following statement? "Employees should be permitted to use social networking sites to communicate with their colleagues in the workplace."

PREPARATION TIME	RESPONSE TIME
00:00:45	00:00:60

MEMO

06

실전유형
모의고사

Question 1-2 : Read a Text Aloud

Directions: In this part of the test, you will read aloud the text on the screen. You will have 45 seconds to prepare. Then you will have 45 seconds to read the text aloud.

Thank you for watching Waterville local news. First, we have your weather news. We will experience chilly and rainy days today and tomorrow. However, when we approach the weekend, we will see several extremely sunny days. Make sure to wear sunscreen, a hat, and sunglasses to protect your skin and eyes.

PREPARATION TIME	RESPONSE TIME
00:00:45	00:00:45

Welcome to the Sweet Surprise Chocolate factory. I hope everybody is excited to get an inside look at the process of manufacturing. During the tour, you will see how chocolates are mixed, molded, and packaged. When we have finished touring the factory, everyone will receive a complimentary assortment of candy.

PREPARATION TIME	RESPONSE TIME
00:00:45	00:00:45

Question 3-4 : Describe a Picture

Directions: In this part of the test, you will describe the picture on your screen in as much detail as you can. You will have 45 seconds to prepare your response. Then you will have 30 seconds to speak about the picture.

PREPARATION TIME	RESPONSE TIME
00:00:45	00:00:30

PREPARATION TIME	RESPONSE TIME
00:00:45	00:00:30

Question 5-7 : Respond to Questions

Directions: In this part of the test, you will answer three questions. You will have three seconds to prepare after you hear each question. You will have 15 seconds to respond to Questions 5 and 6, and 30 seconds to respond to Question 7.

Imagine a magazine publisher is conducting research in your area about organizing family events such as weddings or birthday parties. You have agreed to participate in a telephone interview about organizing family events.

Question 5 of 11

What was the family event you last attended, and where was it held?

PREPARATION TIME	RESPONSE TIME
00:00:03	00:00:15

Question 6 of 11

How much time did you spend attending the last family event, and what kind of food was served?

PREPARATION TIME	RESPONSE TIME
00:00:03	00:00:15

Question 7 of 11

If you were in charge of organizing a family event, what kind of event would you like to hold, and why?

PREPARATION TIME	RESPONSE TIME
00:00:03	00:00:30

Question 8-10 : Respond to Questions Using Information Provided

Directions: In this part of the test, you will answer three questions based on the information provided. You will have 45 seconds to read the information before the questions begin. You will have three seconds to prepare and 15 seconds to respond to Questions 8 and 9. You will hear Question 10 two times. You will have three seconds to prepare and 30 seconds to respond to Question 10.

Wilson Community Center

Spring term: April 3 - May 21, Deadline for registration: March 12

Photography class - basic level	Mondays	2:30 - 3:30 P.M.
Italian cooking: desserts	Tuesdays	1:30 - 2:30 P.M.
Pottery class - advanced level	Wednesdays	4:30 - 5:30 P.M.
Japanese cooking: soups	Thursdays	1:00 - 2:00 P.M.
Water painting	Fridays	2:00 - 3:30 P.M.
Guitar - intermediate level	Saturdays	10:00 - 11:30 A.M.
Costs: 150$ / course (Saturday courses - 100$)		

PREPARATION TIME
00:00:45

Q8

PREPARATION TIME	RESPONSE TIME
00:00:03	00:00:15

Q9

PREPARATION TIME	RESPONSE TIME
00:00:03	00:00:15

Q10

PREPARATION TIME	RESPONSE TIME
00:00:03	00:00:30

Question 11 : Express an Opinion

Directions: In this part of the test, you will give your opinion about a specific topic. Be sure to say as much as you can in the time allowed. You will have 45 seconds to prepare. Then you will have 60 seconds to speak.

For high school students, what are the advantages of acting in theater performances?

PREPARATION TIME	RESPONSE TIME
00:00:45	00:00:60

MEMO

실전유형
모의고사

Question 1-2 : Read a Text Aloud

Directions: In this part of the test, you will read aloud the text on the screen. You will have 45 seconds to prepare. Then you will have 45 seconds to read the text aloud.

This Sunday, visit Jackson Grocery for our tenth-anniversary celebration. Enjoy free dessert, games, and music in the store parking lot. Also, come watch famous chef and cookbook author Pete Evans cook delicious foods. The party starts at 10 A.M. at Jackson Grocery, located at Bank Road, Law Avenue.

PREPARATION TIME	RESPONSE TIME
00:00:45	00:00:45

Hello, and thank you for contacting Samantha's cooking class. We will go through some major renovations for a few weeks. All of our ovens, fridges, and utensils will be replaced. As a result, classes will be closed until the works are finished. To see updates on our progress, please visit our website.

PREPARATION TIME	RESPONSE TIME
00:00:45	00:00:45

Question 3-4 : Describe a Picture

Directions: In this part of the test, you will describe the picture on your screen in as much detail as you can. You will have 45 seconds to prepare your response. Then you will have 30 seconds to speak about the picture.

PREPARATION TIME	RESPONSE TIME
00:00:45	00:00:30

PREPARATION TIME	RESPONSE TIME
00:00:45	00:00:30

Question 5-7 : Respond to Questions

Directions: In this part of the test, you will answer three questions. You will have three seconds to prepare after you hear each question. You will have 15 seconds to respond to Questions 5 and 6, and 30 seconds to respond to Question 7.

Imagine an interior magazine publisher is conducting research in your area about renting a house. You have agreed to participate in a telephone interview about renting a house.

Question 5 of 11

Is it easy to find a house to rent in your area? Why or why not?

PREPARATION TIME	RESPONSE TIME
00:00:03	00:00:15

Question 6 of 11

If you were looking for a house to rent, would you want your friend to visit the house with you, or would you like to go alone, and why?

PREPARATION TIME	RESPONSE TIME
00:00:03	00:00:15

Question 7 of 11

When choosing a house to live in, which of the following is the most important consideration for you and why?

- Whether a shopping center is located nearby or not
- Whether public transportation is close or not
- Whether having pets is allowed or not

PREPARATION TIME	RESPONSE TIME
00:00:03	00:00:30

Question 8-10 : Respond to Questions Using Information Provided

Directions: In this part of the test, you will answer three questions based on the information provided. You will have 45 seconds to read the information before the questions begin. You will have three seconds to prepare and 15 seconds to respond to Questions 8 and 9. You will hear Question 10 two times. You will have three seconds to prepare and 30 seconds to respond to Question 10.

Business association - Quarterly seminar
Daven hotel, Seminar fee: 90$ in advance, 110$ at the seminar

9:30 A.M. - 10:30 A.M.	Registration	-
10:30 A.M. - 11:30 A.M.	Keynote speech: your target audience	Hailey Pitt
11:30 A.M. - 12:30 P.M.	Lecture: importance of customer loyalty	Donald Cho
12:30 P.M. - 1:30 P.M.	Lunch (Buffet - Holly restaurant)	-
1:30 P.M. - 2:30 P.M.	Discussion: marketing trends	Alice Molina
2:30 P.M. - 3:30 P.M.	Workshop: building brand awareness	Donald Cho

PREPARATION TIME
00:00:45

Q8

PREPARATION TIME	RESPONSE TIME
00:00:03	00:00:15

Q9

PREPARATION TIME	RESPONSE TIME
00:00:03	00:00:15

Q10

PREPARATION TIME	RESPONSE TIME
00:00:03	00:00:30

Question 11 : Express an Opinion

Directions: In this part of the test, you will give your opinion about a specific topic. Be sure to say as much as you can in the time allowed. You will have 45 seconds to prepare. Then you will have 60 seconds to speak.

What are the benefits of planning for a trip in advance?

PREPARATION TIME	RESPONSE TIME
00:00:45	00:00:60

MEMO

08

실전유형
모의고사

Question 1-2 : Read a Text Aloud

Directions: In this part of the test, you will read aloud the text on the screen. You will have 45 seconds to prepare. Then you will have 45 seconds to read the text aloud.

In local news, the area restaurant Jay's pizza will be closing next month. Jay Davis, the owner of the restaurant, opened the store thirty years ago. Over the years, it became one of Chicago's most popular places for catering, birthday parties, and other celebrations.

PREPARATION TIME	RESPONSE TIME
00:00:45	00:00:45

Attention commuters. The trains on the red line are fifty minutes behind schedule. If you are traveling on the red line, consider taking an alternative to your destination. Remember, transit passes offer full access to all the trains, buses, and street cars.

PREPARATION TIME	RESPONSE TIME
00:00:45	00:00:45

Question 3-4 : Describe a Picture

Directions: In this part of the test, you will describe the picture on your screen in as much detail as you can. You will have 45 seconds to prepare your response. Then you will have 30 seconds to speak about the picture.

PREPARATION TIME	RESPONSE TIME
00:00:45	00:00:30

PREPARATION TIME	RESPONSE TIME
00:00:45	00:00:30

Question 5-7 : Respond to Questions

Directions: In this part of the test, you will answer three questions. You will have three seconds to prepare after you hear each question. You will have 15 seconds to respond to Questions 5 and 6, and 30 seconds to respond to Question 7.

Imagine a marketing firm is conducting research about health and fitness, and you have agreed to participate in a telephone interview about it.

How often do you exercise, and who do you usually exercise with?

PREPARATION TIME	RESPONSE TIME
00:00:03	00:00:15

What is your favorite type of exercise, and where do you usually do that exercise?

PREPARATION TIME	RESPONSE TIME
00:00:03	00:00:15

What are the advantages of group exercise over working out alone?

PREPARATION TIME	RESPONSE TIME
00:00:03	00:00:30

Question 8-10 : Respond to Questions Using Information Provided

Directions: In this part of the test, you will answer three questions based on the information provided. You will have 45 seconds to read the information before the questions begin. You will have three seconds to prepare and 15 seconds to respond to Questions 8 and 9. You will hear Question 10 two times. You will have three seconds to prepare and 30 seconds to respond to Question 10.

International Conference of Video Game Industry
Friday, March 3, Carol Conference Center

9:00 - 10:00 A.M.	Opening remarks (conference organizer)
10:00 - 11:00 A.M.	Educational video games for class (Room 220)
11:00 A.M. - 12:30 P.M.	Top.10 video games in Asia (Room 110)
12:30 - 1:30 P.M.	Events for games: upcoming events (Room 240)
1:30 - 2:30 P.M.	Lists of gaming conventions (Room 310)
2:30 - 3:30 P.M.	Recent trends on educational video games (Room 115)
3:30 - 5:00 P.M	Outstanding video game developers (Room 410)

PREPARATION TIME
00:00:45

Q8

PREPARATION TIME	RESPONSE TIME
00:00:03	00:00:15

Q9

PREPARATION TIME	RESPONSE TIME
00:00:03	00:00:15

Q10

PREPARATION TIME	RESPONSE TIME
00:00:03	00:00:30

Question 11 : Express an Opinion

Directions: In this part of the test, you will give your opinion about a specific topic. Be sure to say as much as you can in the time allowed. You will have 45 seconds to prepare. Then you will have 60 seconds to speak.

Do you agree that leaders should have strong time-management skills?

PREPARATION TIME	RESPONSE TIME
00:00:45	00:00:60

MEMO

09

실전유형
모의고사

Question 1-2 : Read a Text Aloud

Directions: In this part of the test, you will read aloud the text on the screen. You will have 45 seconds to prepare. Then you will have 45 seconds to read the text aloud.

In today's episode of My Little Kitchen, I will demonstrate how to make delicious tomato soup. To begin, you will need several fresh tomatoes. First, simmer tomatoes, butter, and onion until slightly thickened. Next, add a little water and blend everything together just before serving. I recommend you serve this with a slice of rosemary bread.

PREPARATION TIME	RESPONSE TIME
00:00:45	00:00:45

Good morning, employees. We would like to introduce you to Mr. James Harden, the new chairman of this semiconductor company. In the past, he's held senior positions in many industries including electronics, technology, and automotive. As you may know, he's also been a member of the National Semiconductor Council for three years.

PREPARATION TIME	RESPONSE TIME
00:00:45	00:00:45

Question 3-4 : Describe a Picture

Directions: In this part of the test, you will describe the picture on your screen in as much detail as you can. You will have 45 seconds to prepare your response. Then you will have 30 seconds to speak about the picture.

PREPARATION TIME	RESPONSE TIME
00:00:45	00:00:30

PREPARATION TIME	RESPONSE TIME
00:00:45	00:00:30

Question 5-7 : Respond to Questions

Directions: In this part of the test, you will answer three questions. You will have three seconds to prepare after you hear each question. You will have 15 seconds to respond to Questions 5 and 6, and 30 seconds to respond to Question 7.

Imagine a lifestyle magazine is conducting research in your community about where you live. You have agreed to participate in a telephone interview about it.

Question 5 of 11

Where do you live, and how long have you lived there?

PREPARATION TIME	RESPONSE TIME
00:00:03	00:00:15

Question 6 of 11

Where is the fun place to go in your area, and how often do you go there?

PREPARATION TIME	RESPONSE TIME
00:00:03	00:00:15

Question 7 of 11

When deciding where to live, which of the following is the most important factor, and why?

- Educational Environment
- Access to the public transportation
- Size of the town

PREPARATION TIME	RESPONSE TIME
00:00:03	00:00:30

Question 8-10 : Respond to Questions Using Information Provided

Directions: In this part of the test, you will answer three questions based on the information provided. You will have 45 seconds to read the information before the questions begin. You will have three seconds to prepare and 15 seconds to respond to Questions 8 and 9. You will hear Question 10 two times. You will have three seconds to prepare and 30 seconds to respond to Question 10.

Greenville Park
Events: June - August, Free unless noted

Event	Date	Time
Guided hike: Fame trail	June 15	2:00 - 3:00 P.M.
Family picnic	June 25	10:00 - 11:00 A.M.
Children camp night	July 9	4:00 - 5:00 P.M.
Talk: park history	July 30	1:00 - 2:00 P.M.
Dance competition	August 1	1:00 - 2:00 P.M.
Movie day	August 11	7:30 - 9:30 P.M.
Talk: identifying plants	August 29	3:30 - 4:30 P.M.

PREPARATION TIME
00:00:45

Q8

PREPARATION TIME	RESPONSE TIME
00:00:03	00:00:15

Q9

PREPARATION TIME	RESPONSE TIME
00:00:03	00:00:15

Q10

PREPARATION TIME	RESPONSE TIME
00:00:03	00:00:30

Question 11 : Express an Opinion

Directions: In this part of the test, you will give your opinion about a specific topic. Be sure to say as much as you can in the time allowed. You will have 45 seconds to prepare. Then you will have 60 seconds to speak.

Do you agree or disagree with the following statement?
"Salaries should be determined by skills only but not by how long a person has worked."

PREPARATION TIME	RESPONSE TIME
00:00:45	00:00:60

MEMO

10

실전유형
모의고사

Question 1-2 : Read a Text Aloud

Directions: In this part of the test, you will read aloud the text on the screen. You will have 45 seconds to prepare. Then you will have 45 seconds to read the text aloud.

Question 1 of 11

Thank you for watching Max and Milly's Morning TV show. Today, we will speak with a local musician John Stanley, who uses unusual instruments to create exceptional sounds. But first, let's check on breaking news, weather, and sports.

PREPARATION TIME	RESPONSE TIME
00:00:45	00:00:45

Question 2 of 11

Welcome to the guided walking tour to the Goldstone National Park. During the tour, we will explore the scenic trails, experience the natural amenities, and end with a light outdoor dinner. Before we begin, I want to make sure that everyone is wearing appropriate clothing and footwear.

PREPARATION TIME	RESPONSE TIME
00:00:45	00:00:45

Question 3-4 : Describe a Picture

Directions: In this part of the test, you will describe the picture on your screen in as much detail as you can. You will have 45 seconds to prepare your response. Then you will have 30 seconds to speak about the picture.

PREPARATION TIME	RESPONSE TIME
00:00:45	00:00:30

PREPARATION TIME	RESPONSE TIME
00:00:45	00:00:30

Question 5-7 : Respond to Questions

Directions: In this part of the test, you will answer three questions. You will have three seconds to prepare after you hear each question. You will have 15 seconds to respond to Questions 5 and 6, and 30 seconds to respond to Question 7.

Imagine a marketing firm is conducting research in your area about life patterns. You have agreed to participate in a telephone interview about it.

Question 5 of 11

What time does your work or school start? What time does it end?

PREPARATION TIME	RESPONSE TIME
00:00:03	00:00:15

Question 6 of 11

Do you keep track of important schedules on your note or an electronic device, and why?

PREPARATION TIME	RESPONSE TIME
00:00:03	00:00:15

Question 7 of 11

If an opportunity to change the time your workday or school day starts and ends is given, would you? Why or why not?

PREPARATION TIME	RESPONSE TIME
00:00:03	00:00:30

Question 8-10 : Respond to Questions Using Information Provided

Directions: In this part of the test, you will answer three questions based on the information provided. You will have 45 seconds to read the information before the questions begin. You will have three seconds to prepare and 15 seconds to respond to Questions 8 and 9. You will hear Question 10 two times. You will have three seconds to prepare and 30 seconds to respond to Question 10.

Sales Employees Association Meeting
City Electronics / November 2 / Employee Lounge

9:00 - 10:00 A.M.	Breakfast	-
10:00 - 11:00 A.M.	Employee Orientation	Rose Kinder
11:00 A.M. - Noon	Store tour	James Aron
Noon - 1:00 P.M.	Lunch	-
1:00 - 2:00 P.M.	Video: customer satisfaction (Includes quizzes for trainees)	Brad Tailor
2:00 - 3:00 P.M.	Lecture: customer-driven mind	Akiko Nami
3:00 - 4:00 P.M.	Video: communication skills (Includes networking)	Nina Simon

PREPARATION TIME

00:00:45

Q8

PREPARATION TIME	RESPONSE TIME
00:00:03	00:00:15

Q9

PREPARATION TIME	RESPONSE TIME
00:00:03	00:00:15

Q10

PREPARATION TIME	RESPONSE TIME
00:00:03	00:00:30

Question 11 : Express an Opinion

Directions: In this part of the test, you will give your opinion about a specific topic. Be sure to say as much as you can in the time allowed. You will have 45 seconds to prepare. Then you will have 60 seconds to speak.

Is it important for a team leader to have skills for managing conflicts?

PREPARATION TIME	RESPONSE TIME
00:00:45	00:00:60

MEMO

11

실전유형
모의고사

Question 1-2 : Read a Text Aloud

Directions: In this part of the test, you will read aloud the text on the screen. You will have 45 seconds to prepare. Then you will have 45 seconds to read the text aloud.

Hello and welcome back to our Talk Show. We'll be interviewing a famous rock band, known for their energetic live performances. The group is made up of a guitarist, drummer, and singer. After the interview, they will play a song from the latest release.

PREPARATION TIME	RESPONSE TIME
00:00:45	00:00:45

Welcome to the gardening class. Beginning in a few minutes, the expert gardener Davis Mill will give a talk on designing gardens. He will talk about designing small gardens, the history of garden design, and a farmer's life. Afterward, he will answer any questions you may have.

PREPARATION TIME	RESPONSE TIME
00:00:45	00:00:45

Question 3-4 : Describe a Picture

Directions: In this part of the test, you will describe the picture on your screen in as much detail as you can. You will have 45 seconds to prepare your response. Then you will have 30 seconds to speak about the picture.

PREPARATION TIME	RESPONSE TIME
00:00:45	00:00:30

PREPARATION TIME	RESPONSE TIME
00:00:45	00:00:30

Question 5-7 : Respond to Questions

Directions: In this part of the test, you will answer three questions. You will have three seconds to prepare after you hear each question. You will have 15 seconds to respond to Questions 5 and 6, and 30 seconds to respond to Question 7.

Imagine you're talking on the phone with your friend about having parties.

Question 5 of 11

When was the last time you went to a housewarming party and where was it?

PREPARATION TIME	RESPONSE TIME
00:00:03	00:00:15

Question 6 of 11

When you go to a party, do you usually bring a gift for a host?

PREPARATION TIME	RESPONSE TIME
00:00:03	00:00:15

Question 7 of 11

If you were the host of the party, would you plan activities? Why or why not?

PREPARATION TIME	RESPONSE TIME
00:00:03	00:00:30

Question 8-10 : Respond to Questions Using Information Provided

Directions: In this part of the test, you will answer three questions based on the information provided. You will have 45 seconds to read the information before the questions begin. You will have three seconds to prepare and 15 seconds to respond to Questions 8 and 9. You will hear Question 10 two times. You will have three seconds to prepare and 30 seconds to respond to Question 10.

Question 8-10 of 11

Professional Development Seminar for Art Teachers
Central Conference Hall, January 15

Time	Session	Speaker
9:00 - 10:00 A.M.	On-site registration	-
10:00 - 11:00 A.M.	Lecture: Preparing students for Art University	Brian Owen
11:00 A.M. - Noon	Workshop: Principles of artful teaching	Johnson Veronica
Noon - 1:00 P.M.	Lunch (Tillet dining hall)	-
1:00 - 2:00 P.M.	Workshop: Developing students as artists	Simon Thomas
2:00 - 3:00 P.M.	Presentation: Virtual art education	Collin Firth

PREPARATION TIME
00:00:45

Q8

PREPARATION TIME	RESPONSE TIME
00:00:03	00:00:15

Q9

PREPARATION TIME	RESPONSE TIME
00:00:03	00:00:15

Q10

PREPARATION TIME	RESPONSE TIME
00:00:03	00:00:30

Question 11 : Express an Opinion

Directions: In this part of the test, you will give your opinion about a specific topic. Be sure to say as much as you can in the time allowed. You will have 45 seconds to prepare. Then you will have 60 seconds to speak.

Do you agree or disagree with the following statement?
"It is important to have outdoor playtime during school time."

PREPARATION TIME	RESPONSE TIME
00:00:45	00:00:60

MEMO

12

실전유형
모의고사

Question 1-2 : Read a Text Aloud

Directions: In this part of the test, you will read aloud the text on the screen. You will have 45 seconds to prepare. Then you will have 45 seconds to read the text aloud.

Welcome to Peter's Park. On today's tour, we will walk through a beautiful collection of plants and flowers. Through the property, you'll see many varieties of daisies, roses, and tulips. While enjoying the tour, please feel free to take photographs.

PREPARATION TIME	RESPONSE TIME
00:00:45	00:00:45

We're thrilled to announce the grand opening of a new bar in Frankland city. Though everyone can find what they like, the Whitehouse is mainly a wine bar. The menu includes cheese boards, salmon pasta, and grilled chicken. What's more, we have a fantastic children's menu. Make your reservation today.

PREPARATION TIME	RESPONSE TIME
00:00:45	00:00:45

Question 3-4 : Describe a Picture

Directions: In this part of the test, you will describe the picture on your screen in as much detail as you can. You will have 45 seconds to prepare your response. Then you will have 30 seconds to speak about the picture.

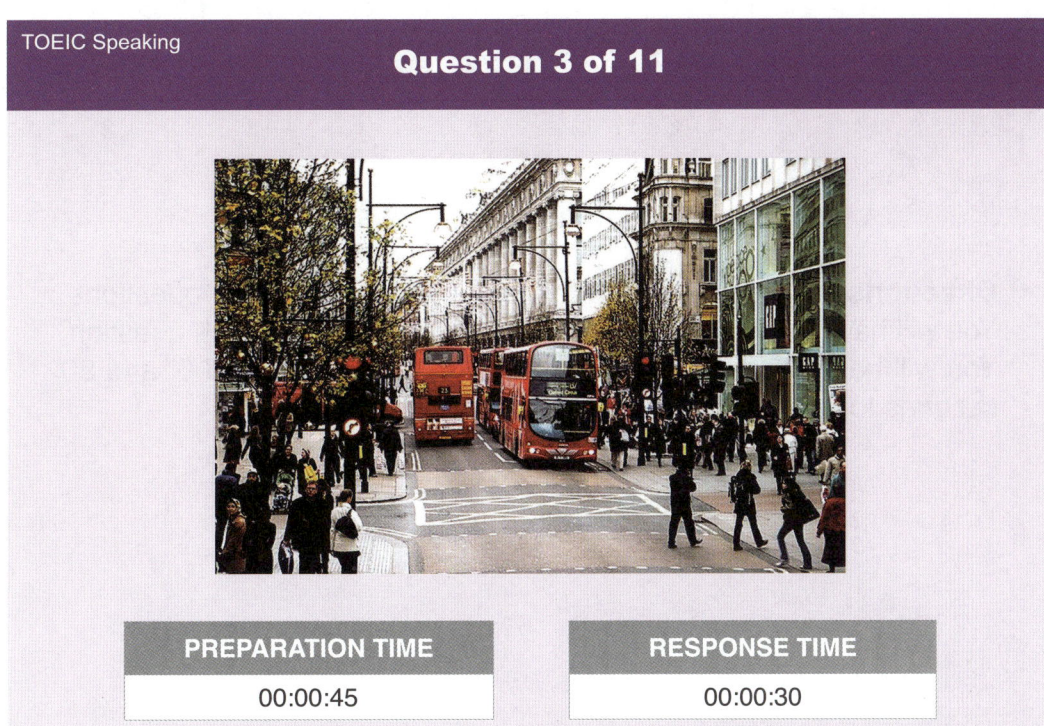

PREPARATION TIME		RESPONSE TIME
00:00:45		00:00:30

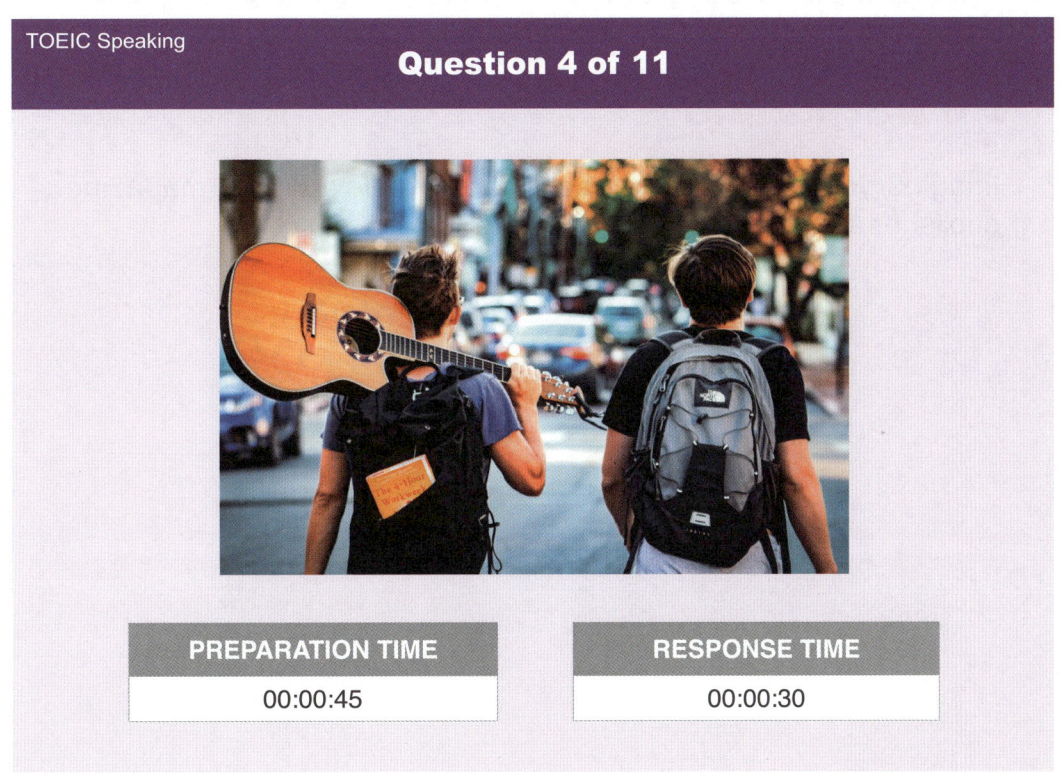

PREPARATION TIME		RESPONSE TIME
00:00:45		00:00:30

Question 5-7 : Respond to Questions

Directions: In this part of the test, you will answer three questions. You will have three seconds to prepare after you hear each question. You will have 15 seconds to respond to Questions 5 and 6, and 30 seconds to respond to Question 7.

Imagine you are having a telephone interview with a magazine publisher about work.

What do you do for work, or if you're a student, what do you study?

PREPARATION TIME	RESPONSE TIME
00:00:03	00:00:15

Do you think the location of a company is important? Why or why not?

PREPARATION TIME	RESPONSE TIME
00:00:03	00:00:15

Which of the following is the most important factor when getting a job?

- Opportunities for promotion
- Good employee benefits
- The availability of a flexible schedule

PREPARATION TIME	RESPONSE TIME
00:00:03	00:00:30

Question 8-10 : Respond to Questions Using Information Provided

Directions: In this part of the test, you will answer three questions based on the information provided. You will have 45 seconds to read the information before the questions begin. You will have three seconds to prepare and 15 seconds to respond to Questions 8 and 9. You will hear Question 10 two times. You will have three seconds to prepare and 30 seconds to respond to Question 10.

Genie's Art Classes

Santa Ana art center: Main classroom, Fall semester: October 3 - November 2
Fee: membership 20$, non-membership 30$

Pencil drawing	Mondays	9:00 - 10:00 A.M.
Draw and sketch	Tuesdays	10:00 - 11:00 A.M.
Digital sketching for beginners	Tuesdays	11:00 A.M. - Noon
Watercolor painting for beginners	Wednesdays	2:00 - 3:30 P.M.
Figure drawing	Fridays	1:00 - 2:00 P.M.
Sculpture	Saturdays	7:30 - 9:30 P.M.

PREPARATION TIME
00:00:45

Q8

PREPARATION TIME	RESPONSE TIME
00:00:03	00:00:15

Q9

PREPARATION TIME	RESPONSE TIME
00:00:03	00:00:15

Q10

PREPARATION TIME	RESPONSE TIME
00:00:03	00:00:30

Question 11 : Express an Opinion

Directions: In this part of the test, you will give your opinion about a specific topic. Be sure to say as much as you can in the time allowed. You will have 45 seconds to prepare. Then you will have 60 seconds to speak.

Do you agree or disagree with the following statement?
"It is necessary for teachers to attend training workshops each year."

PREPARATION TIME	RESPONSE TIME
00:00:45	00:00:60

MEMO

13

실전유형
모의고사

Question 1-2 : Read a Text Aloud

Directions: In this part of the test, you will read aloud the text on the screen. You will have 45 seconds to prepare. Then you will have 45 seconds to read the text aloud.

Question 1 of 11

Welcome to Channel Twelve weather news. The snow that started yesterday will continue throughout the day. Sunday, however, conditions will improve with warmer temperatures, clear skies, and a light breeze. If you are interested in how today's weather affects traffic, stay tuned, because the traffic news is next.

PREPARATION TIME	RESPONSE TIME
00:00:45	00:00:45

Question 2 of 11

Thank you for attending this writing seminar. Today, we will start with a workshop led by Erick Sharon, a writing instructor at the local community center. Mr. Sharon is also a famous writer. His third fiction Red Night has just been published this year. During the workshop, he'll be discussing how to develop fiction elements of plot, setting, character, and conflict.

PREPARATION TIME	RESPONSE TIME
00:00:45	00:00:45

Question 3-4 : Describe a Picture

Directions: In this part of the test, you will describe the picture on your screen in as much detail as you can. You will have 45 seconds to prepare your response. Then you will have 30 seconds to speak about the picture.

PREPARATION TIME	RESPONSE TIME
00:00:45	00:00:30

PREPARATION TIME	RESPONSE TIME
00:00:45	00:00:30

Question 5-7 : Respond to Questions

Directions: In this part of the test, you will answer three questions. You will have three seconds to prepare after you hear each question. You will have 15 seconds to respond to Questions 5 and 6, and 30 seconds to respond to Question 7.

Imagine a lifestyle magazine is conducting research in your area about cleaning your room. You have agreed to participate in a telephone interview about it.

Question 5 of 11

Who does most of the cleaning of your room, and why?

PREPARATION TIME	RESPONSE TIME
00:00:03	00:00:15

Question 6 of 11

Do you spend more time cleaning your room than you did five years ago? Why or why not?

PREPARATION TIME	RESPONSE TIME
00:00:03	00:00:15

Question 7 of 11

If you clean your room, would you start with the easiest task or with the most difficult one, and why?

PREPARATION TIME	RESPONSE TIME
00:00:03	00:00:30

Question 8-10 : Respond to Questions Using Information Provided

Directions: In this part of the test, you will answer three questions based on the information provided. You will have 45 seconds to read the information before the questions begin. You will have three seconds to prepare and 15 seconds to respond to Questions 8 and 9. You will hear Question 10 two times. You will have three seconds to prepare and 30 seconds to respond to Question 10.

TOEIC Speaking

Library Management Conference
Hiller's hall, room 201, October 3

Schedule	
9:00 - 10:00 A.M.	President's speech
10:00 - 11:00 A.M.	Lecture: qualified librarians
11:00 A.M. - Noon	Workshop: management of children's book section
Noon - 1:00 P.M.	Buffet lunch
1:00 - 2:00 P.M.	Group discussion: films for children
2:00 - 3:00 P.M.	Presentation: issues with old books
3:00 - 4:00 P.M.	Award ceremony: best librarians of this year

PREPARATION TIME
00:00:45

Q8

PREPARATION TIME	RESPONSE TIME
00:00:03	00:00:15

Q9

PREPARATION TIME	RESPONSE TIME
00:00:03	00:00:15

Q10

PREPARATION TIME	RESPONSE TIME
00:00:03	00:00:30

Question 11 : Express an Opinion

Directions: In this part of the test, you will give your opinion about a specific topic. Be sure to say as much as you can in the time allowed. You will have 45 seconds to prepare. Then you will have 60 seconds to speak.

Which is more important for a salesperson's success: having social skills or having extensive knowledge of products being sold?

PREPARATION TIME	RESPONSE TIME
00:00:45	00:00:60

MEMO

14

실전유형
모의고사

Question 1-2 : Read a Text Aloud

Directions: In this part of the test, you will read aloud the text on the screen. You will have 45 seconds to prepare. Then you will have 45 seconds to read the text aloud.

If you are looking for summer activities for your teenagers, check out Park Hill community center. This summer, Park Hill community center will offer programs in volunteering, media, and career. These programs are specifically designed for teenagers and will be able to accommodate any skill level. For more information on programs, please visit our website.

PREPARATION TIME	RESPONSE TIME
00:00:45	00:00:45

Attention, passengers. This is the express bus to Albertson Ville. Please note that we're not going to stop at Billington station, which is currently under construction. Before you exit the bus, please make sure to take any bags, small electronic devices, and other personal belongings. Thank you for traveling with us today.

PREPARATION TIME	RESPONSE TIME
00:00:45	00:00:45

Question 3-4 : Describe a Picture

Directions: In this part of the test, you will describe the picture on your screen in as much detail as you can. You will have 45 seconds to prepare your response. Then you will have 30 seconds to speak about the picture.

PREPARATION TIME	RESPONSE TIME
00:00:45	00:00:30

PREPARATION TIME	RESPONSE TIME
00:00:45	00:00:30

Question 5-7 : Respond to Questions

Directions: In this part of the test, you will answer three questions. You will have three seconds to prepare after you hear each question. You will have 15 seconds to respond to Questions 5 and 6, and 30 seconds to respond to Question 7.

Imagine a travel magazine publisher is conducting research about traveling. You have agreed to participate in a telephone interview about it.

TOEIC Speaking

Question 5 of 11

Do you like to read travel articles? Why or why not?

PREPARATION TIME	RESPONSE TIME
00:00:03	00:00:15

TOEIC Speaking

Question 6 of 11

When was the last time you traveled abroad, and who did you travel with?

PREPARATION TIME	RESPONSE TIME
00:00:03	00:00:15

TOEIC Speaking

Question 7 of 11

When traveling abroad, do you prefer to travel throughout the countryside or travel to the city?

PREPARATION TIME	RESPONSE TIME
00:00:03	00:00:30

Question 8-10 : Respond to Questions Using Information Provided

Directions: In this part of the test, you will answer three questions based on the information provided. You will have 45 seconds to read the information before the questions begin. You will have three seconds to prepare and 15 seconds to respond to Questions 8 and 9. You will hear Question 10 two times. You will have three seconds to prepare and 30 seconds to respond to Question 10.

Palm State University	
George Stephan, President, December 2	
9:00 - 10:00 A.M.	President's speech
10:00 - 11:00 A.M.	Presentation: Career and further studies
11:00 A.M. - Noon	Committee meeting: Academic affairs, Room 12
Noon - 1:00 P.M.	Lunch (Phillip Kim, vice president)
1:00 - 2:00 P.M.	Lecture: International law class
2:00 - 3:00 P.M.	Committee meeting: Finance, Conference room A
3:00 - 4:00 P.M.	Social hour: Student-award recipients

PREPARATION TIME
00:00:45

Q8

PREPARATION TIME	RESPONSE TIME
00:00:03	00:00:15

Q9

PREPARATION TIME	RESPONSE TIME
00:00:03	00:00:15

Q10

PREPARATION TIME	RESPONSE TIME
00:00:03	00:00:30

Question 11 : Express an Opinion

Directions: In this part of the test, you will give your opinion about a specific topic. Be sure to say as much as you can in the time allowed. You will have 45 seconds to prepare. Then you will have 60 seconds to speak.

Do you agree or disagree with the following statement?
"Reading a book relaxes you more than exercising."

PREPARATION TIME	RESPONSE TIME
00:00:45	00:00:60

MEMO

15

실전유형
모의고사

Question 1-2 : Read a Text Aloud

Directions: In this part of the test, you will read aloud the text on the screen. You will have 45 seconds to prepare. Then you will have 45 seconds to read the text aloud.

Question 1 of 11

Welcome to the guided tour. You are now at the main gallery of the British Museum. In front of you is a replica of a plane, Brave Lion, built forty years ago, and this small airplane was designed by Peter Strokes. This plane has a relatively small wingspan, two-hundred-gallon fuel capacity, and seating for five passengers.

PREPARATION TIME	RESPONSE TIME
00:00:45	00:00:45

Question 2 of 11

This Sunday, the staff members of The Aussie Grill will invite you and your family to our restaurant. We open twenty-four hours a day, and breakfast, lunch, and dinner are always available. If you arrive before noon, don't forget to ask a staff member for free drinks.

PREPARATION TIME	RESPONSE TIME
00:00:45	00:00:45

Question 3-4 : Describe a Picture

Directions: In this part of the test, you will describe the picture on your screen in as much detail as you can. You will have 45 seconds to prepare your response. Then you will have 30 seconds to speak about the picture.

PREPARATION TIME	RESPONSE TIME
00:00:45	00:00:30

PREPARATION TIME	RESPONSE TIME
00:00:45	00:00:30

Question 5-7 : Respond to Questions

Directions: In this part of the test, you will answer three questions. You will have three seconds to prepare after you hear each question. You will have 15 seconds to respond to Questions 5 and 6, and 30 seconds to respond to Question 7.

Imagine a marketing firm is conducting research about streaming services that allow you to watch movies without downloading them first. You have agreed to participate in a telephone interview about it.

Question 5 of 11

How often do you watch movies, and where do you usually watch them?

PREPARATION TIME	RESPONSE TIME
00:00:03	00:00:15

Question 6 of 11

Would you be willing to pay for streaming services to watch movies? Why or why not?

PREPARATION TIME	RESPONSE TIME
00:00:03	00:00:15

Question 7 of 11

Which of the following is the most important factor when choosing a movie on a streaming service?

- Viewers' ratings
- Genre
- Reviews written by famous critics

PREPARATION TIME	RESPONSE TIME
00:00:03	00:00:30

Question 8-10 : Respond to Questions Using Information Provided

Directions: In this part of the test, you will answer three questions based on the information provided. You will have 45 seconds to read the information before the questions begin. You will have three seconds to prepare and 15 seconds to respond to Questions 8 and 9. You will hear Question 10 two times. You will have three seconds to prepare and 30 seconds to respond to Question 10.

Yorktown Community Center One-day class
November 2, Symbol community center

Simple baking	10:00 - 11:30 A.M.	Allen Phillip	Room A
Irish dance	2:00 - 3:30 P.M.	Rose Moore	Main Hall
Japanese cooking	3:30 - 4:30 P.M.	Jason Molina	Room C
Zumba dance	4:30 - 5:00 P.M.	Nicole Kimberly	Room A
Introduction of painting	5:00 - 6:30 P.M.	~~Michael Phillip~~ *Changed to Alan Bell*	Main Hall
Drawing	7:00 - 8:30 P.M.	Kevin Stella	Main Hall

PREPARATION TIME
00:00:45

Q8

PREPARATION TIME	RESPONSE TIME
00:00:03	00:00:15

Q9

PREPARATION TIME	RESPONSE TIME
00:00:03	00:00:15

Q10

PREPARATION TIME	RESPONSE TIME
00:00:03	00:00:30

Question 11 : Express an Opinion

Directions: In this part of the test, you will give your opinion about a specific topic. Be sure to say as much as you can in the time allowed. You will have 45 seconds to prepare. Then you will have 60 seconds to speak.

Do you agree or disagree with the following statement? "Employees have more work done when they have flexible schedules."

PREPARATION TIME	RESPONSE TIME
00:00:45	00:00:60

MEMO

인강
벼락치기
템플릿

토익스피킹 MUST HAVE

평생패스

❝
등급별 멀티 템플릿이 수록된
제인토스 인강
❞

여러 문제에 적용할 수 있는
등급별(IM-AH) 멀티 템플릿이
수록된 인강으로 실전 감각을
극대화 할 수 있습니다.

❝
최신 출제 트렌드를 반영한
실전 유형 자료
❞

매월 극최신 실전유형자료 4회분으로
유사 문제 유형을 대비하고 모범 답안 템플릿을
통해 부족한 점을 보완할 수 있습니다.

❝
Part 3,5 최빈출 문제만 모은
벼락치기 템플릿
❞

토스 시험 점수의 등락을 결정짓는 Part 3,5
최빈출 주제와 등급별 답안 템플릿을
한눈에 비교할 수 있어 등급 정체 구간도
문제없이 뚫을 수 있습니다.

❝
목표 등급에 따라 만드는
마이 템플릿
❞

인강과 라이브 클래스 VOD, 벼락치기 템플릿에
수록된 목표 등급에 따른 모범 답안을 참고하여
만든 나만의 템플릿을 활용할 수 있습니다.

'네이버'에서 제인토스를 검색하세요.

| 제인토스 ▼ | 검색 |

멱살잡고 캐리하는

줄빡공스터디

대한민국 유일의
토익스피킹 LIVE클래스

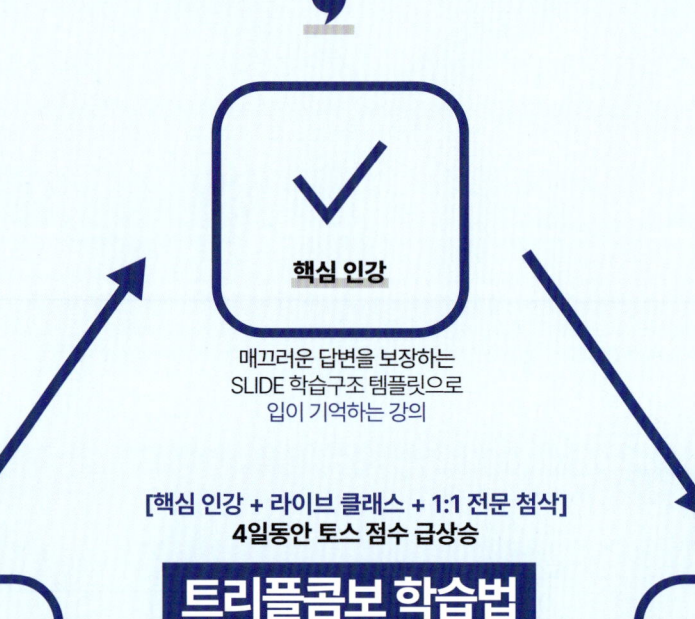

핵심 인강

매끄러운 답변을 보장하는
SLIDE 학습구조 템플릿으로
입이 기억하는 강의

[핵심 인강 + 라이브 클래스 + 1:1 전문 첨삭]
4일동안 토스 점수 급상승

트리플콤보 학습법

1:1 전문 첨삭

입으로 완성한 답변
정확한 첨삭으로
구체적인 실력진단
및 강약점 파악

라이브 클래스

SLIDE 학습 구조 템플릿
암기+말하기로
입이 트이는
실시간 온라인 스터디

5일 완성
토익스피킹
멀티템플릿
실전북

IM-AH

모범답변 · 템플릿

제인토스
Study With Teacher

01

실전유형 모의고사

모범답변·템플릿

Question 1

Starting this week, →/ Cake Lady will be offering brand new cheesecakes. ↘// In addition to the standard selection, →/ we're glad to introduce carrot, ↗/red velvet, ↗/ and hazelnut flavors. ↘// To sample the brand-new flavors, →/ be sure to stop by our shop →/ on Mandarine avenue. ↘//

이번 주를 시작으로, 케이크 레이디는 새로운 치즈케이크를 제공할 것입니다. 기본 메뉴들 외에 당근, 레드 벨벳, 그리고 헤이즐넛 맛도 소개하게 되어 기쁩니다. 새로운 맛들을 맛보려면, 맨다린 애비뉴에 있는 저희 가게에 들러보세요.

Question 2

Thanks for tuning in →/ to Kingsville's morning traffic report. ↘// Because of the electronics convention downtown, →/ driving on several main roads →/ will be slower than usual. ↘// For alternatives, →/ we suggest riding a subway, ↗/ taking a bus ↗/ or walking. ↘// For those of you →/ who will be driving, →/ stay tuned for more details →/ on recommended routes. ↘//

킹스빌 아침 교통 정보를 청취해 주셔서 감사합니다. 시내에서 열리는 전자제품 컨벤션 때문에 몇몇 주요 도로에서 주행이 평소보다 느려질 것입니다. 대안으로는 지하철이나 버스를 타거나 걷는 것을 권해드립니다. 운전하실 분들은 추천경로에 대한 더 자세한 정보를 원하신다면 채널 고정해 주세요.

Question 3

장소	This picture was taken outdoors.	이 사진은 야외에서 찍힌 사진입니다.

인원	There are three people in the scene.	이 장면에는 세 사람이 있습니다.

중심 대상	In the center, two men are carrying a couch to a white car. Next to them, a woman is looking at them.	중앙에는 두 남자가 흰색 자동차로 소파를 옮기고 있습니다. 그들 옆에는 한 여자가 그들을 지켜보고 있습니다.

주변 대상	In the background, I can see trees, houses, and a blue sky.	배경에는 나무, 집 그리고 파란 하늘이 보입니다.

상황	Overall, it seems like two men are helping her carry the couch.	전반적으로 두 남자가 여자가 소파를 옮기는 것을 도와주고 있는 것처럼 보입니다.

Question 4

| 장소 | This picture was taken at an office. | 이 사진은 사무실에서 찍힌 사진입니다. |

| 인원 | There are three people. | 세 명이 있습니다. |

| 중심 대상 | On the left, a woman is pointing at something on the paper and explaining it to the couple. The couple is listening attentively. | 왼쪽에는 여자가 종이에 무언가를 가리키며 커플에게 설명하고 있습니다. 그 커플은 주의 깊게 듣고 있습니다. |

| 주변 대상 | On the desk, there are flowers, a laptop, a phone, and a pencil holder. | 책상 위에는 꽃, 노트북, 전화기, 연필꽂이가 있습니다. |

| 상황 | Overall, it seems like the couple came in for counseling. | 전반적으로 이 커플은 상담을 받으러 온 것 같습니다. |

🔊 Imagine that an Australian marketing firm is conducting research in your area. You have agreed to participate in a telephone interview about shopping for clothes.

한 호주의 마케팅 회사가 당신의 지역에서 연구를 수행하고 있다고 가정해보십시오. 당신은 옷 쇼핑에 관련된 전화 인터뷰에 참여하기로 동의했습니다.

Question 5

Q When was the last time you shopped for clothes, and what did you buy?

당신은 언제 마지막으로 옷을 샀고, 무엇을 샀습니까?

A The last time I shopped for clothes was last month and I bought jeans.

제가 마지막으로 옷을 샀던 것은 지난달이며, 청바지를 샀습니다.

Question 6

Q Besides price, what is the most important consideration for you when deciding which clothes to buy, and why?

가격을 제외하고, 어떤 옷을 살지 결정할 때 당신에게 가장 중요한 고려 사항은 무엇이며, 그 이유는 무엇인가요?

A Besides price, I consider its durability the most. I want to wear clothes as long as I can.

가격을 제외하고, 옷의 내구성을 가장 고려합니다. 저는 가능한 한 옷을 오래 입고 싶습니다.

Q If you were going to buy athletic wear, would you rather go to a sporting goods store or a regular clothing store, and why?

만약 당신이 운동복을 살 것이라면 당신은 스포츠 용품 가게와 일반 옷 가게 중 어디로 가고 싶고, 그 이유는 무엇입니까?

IM3-IH In this case, I would go to a sporting goods store, and here is why. <u>They offer more options to choose from</u>. That is because a sporting goods store sells athletic products only. Therefore, <u>I can buy exactly what I want</u>.
This is why.

이러한 경우에 저는 스포츠 용품점에 갈 것이고, 여기 그 이유가 있습니다.
그들은 선택할 수 있는 더 많은 옵션을 제공합니다. 그것은 스포츠 용품점에서는 운동 용품만 팔기 때문입니다. 그러므로 저는 제가 정확히 원하는 것을 살 수 있습니다.
이것이 그 이유입니다.

AL-AH If I made a choice, I would go to a sporting goods store, and here is why.

First, <u>they offer more options to choose from</u> compared to a regular clothing store. That is because a sporting goods store sells athletic products only. Therefore, <u>I can buy exactly what I want</u>.

Also, the staff members of a sporting goods store have better knowledge of sportswear, which will help me choose the right one.

This is why.

만약 제가 선택을 한다면 저는 스포츠 용품점에 갈 것이고, 여기 그 이유가 있습니다.

첫째, 그들은 일반 옷 가게에 비해 선택할 수 있는 더 많은 옵션을 제공합니다. 왜냐하면 스포츠 용품점에서는 운동 용품만 팔기 때문입니다. 그러므로 저는 제가 정확히 원하는 것을 살 수 있습니다.

또한, 스포츠 용품점의 직원들은 스포츠 의류에 대해 더 잘 알고 있고, 이것은 제가 적절한 것을 고르는데 도움을 줄 것입니다.

이것이 그 이유입니다.

Orange corporation
Marketing team manager, Jim Parker / Itinerary for business trip

Depart Beijing, Vase airlines, flight 127 Arrive Seoul	2:15 P.M. 4:00 P.M.	April 16 April 16
Depart Seoul, Vase airlines, flight 516 Arrive Beijing (lunch provided in the flight)	1:50 P.M. 3:05 P.M.	April 21 April 21
[Accommodation] Central view hotel, room 203 (non-smoking)	Check-in 2:00 P.M. Check-out 11:00 A.M.	April 16-21
[Car rental] Car delivered to Central view hotel Return to the Mobeez rental office	4:00 P.M. 5:00 P.M.	April 16 April 21

🔊 Hi, this is Jim Parker. Can I ask a few questions about my itinerary for a business trip to Seoul in April?

안녕하세요. 저는 짐 파커입니다. 4월에 서울로 가는 제 출장 일정에 대해 몇 가지 물어봐도 될까요?

Question 8

Q What time am I departing from Beijing? Also, I need my flight information.

저는 베이징에서 몇 시에 출국하나요? 그리고 저는 제 항공편 정보가 필요합니다.

A You are departing from Beijing at 2:15 P.M. on April 16th and you will use Vase airlines, flight 127.

당신은 베이징에서 4월 16일 오후 2시 15분에 출국하고 베이스 항공사의 항공편 127을 이용할 것입니다.

Question 9

Q I heard that I will use a rent car during my business trip in Seoul. What time do I have to pick up the rent car?

제가 한국에서 출장을 다니는 동안에 렌터카를 사용할 것이라고 들었습니다. 몇 시에 렌터카를 가지러 가야 하나요?

A Actually, you don't need to pick up the rent car because it will be delivered to your hotel by 4 P.M. on April 16th.

사실 당신은 렌터카를 가지러 가지 않아도 됩니다. 왜냐하면 4월 16일 오후 4시에 당신의 호텔로 전달될 것이기 때문입니다.

Question 10

Q Could you give me all the details of my return trip?

제 돌아오는 일정에 대한 모든 세부사항을 알려 주시겠습니까?

A Sure. First, you will depart from Seoul with Vase airlines, flight 516 at 1:50 P.M. on April 21st. Second, you will arrive in Beijing at 3:05 P.M. on the same day and lunch will be provided in the flight.

물론이죠. 먼저, 당신은 4월 21일 오후 1시 50분에 베이스 항공사의 항공편 516을 타고 서울에서 출국할 것입니다. 두 번째로, 당신은 베이징에 같은 날 오후 3시 5분에 도착할 것이고 점심은 비행기에서 제공될 것입니다.

Question 11

🔊 Do you agree or disagree with the following statement?
"The best way to relieve work-related stress is having a trip." Give reasons or examples to support your opinion.

다음 명제에 동의하십니까, 동의하지 않으십니까?
"업무와 관련된 스트레스를 해소하는 가장 좋은 방법은 여행을 하는 것이다." 당신의 의견을 뒷받침할 이유나 예를 들어주세요.

IM3   I agree that the best way to reduce work-related stress is by having a trip. There are some reasons for this.

First, it's refreshing. By having a trip, they can take a mental break and escape from daily routines.

Second, they can have time to look back on themselves. They will have time to figure out what stresses them out and deal with it.

These are the reasons.

업무와 관련된 스트레스를 해소하는 가장 좋은 방법은 여행을 하는 것이라는 데 동의합니다. 여기에는 몇 가지 이유가 있습니다.

첫째, 기분전환이 됩니다. 여행을 하는 동안 정신적인 휴식을 취할 수 있고 평범한 일상에서 벗어날 수 있습니다.

둘째, 자신을 돌아볼 수 있는 시간을 가질 수 있습니다. 그들은 무엇을 스트레스로 느끼는지를 파악하고 그것을 처리할 시간을 가질 수 있습니다.

이것들이 이유입니다.

I agree that the best way to reduce work-related stress is by having a trip. There are some reasons for this.

First, it's refreshing. By having a trip, they can take a mental break and escape from daily routines. They can get back to work with a positive mindset.

Second, they can have time to look back on themselves. They will have time to figure out what stresses them out and deal with it to reduce their stress level.

These are the reasons.

업무와 관련된 스트레스를 해소하는 가장 좋은 방법은 여행을 하는 것이라는 데 동의합니다. 여기에는 몇 가지 이유가 있습니다.

첫째, 기분전환이 됩니다. 여행을 하는 동안 정신적인 휴식을 취할 수 있고 평범한 일상에서 벗어날 수 있습니다. 그들은 긍정적인 마음으로 다시 일할 수 있습니다.

둘째, 자신을 돌아볼 수 있는 시간을 가질 수 있습니다. 예를 들어 직장과의 격리는 그들이 무엇을 스트레스로 느끼는지를 파악하고 그것을 처리하여 스트레스 수준을 낮출 수 있게 해줍니다.

이것들이 이유입니다.

I agree that the best way to reduce work-related stress is by having a trip. There are some reasons for this.

First, by having a trip, they can take a mental break and escape from daily routines. It will refresh their minds and help them get back to work with a positive mindset.

Second, they can have time to look back on themselves. For instance, isolation from the workplace enables them to figure out what stresses them out and deal with it to reduce their stress level.

These are the reasons.

업무와 관련된 스트레스를 해소하는 가장 좋은 방법은 여행을 하는 것이라는 데 동의합니다. 여기에는 몇 가지 이유가 있습니다.

첫째, 여행을 하는 동안 정신적인 휴식을 취할 수 있고 평범한 일상에서 벗어날 수 있습니다. 이것은 그들을 기분전환 시켜주고 긍정적인 마음으로 다시 일할 수 있도록 도와줄 것입니다.

둘째, 자신을 돌아볼 수 있는 시간을 가질 수 있습니다. 예를 들어 직장과의 격리는 그들이 무엇을 스트레스로 느끼는지를 파악하고 그것을 처리하여 스트레스 수준을 낮출 수 있게 해줍니다.

이것들이 이유입니다.

02 실전유형 모의고사

모범답변·템플릿

Thank you for calling Mandio's, →/ the most popular restaurant in the city. ↘// We will be with you shortly →/ to take your order →/ for your favorite burger, ↗/ sandwich, ↗/ or salad. ↘// For faster services, →/ you can order online →/ on our website. ↘// Also, →/ our website provides specific details →/ about our special items. ↘//

시내에서 가장 인기있는 레스토랑 Mandio's에 전화 주셔서 감사합니다. 당신이 가장 좋아하는 버거, 샌드위치, 샐러드 주문을 받기 위해 곧 연결될 것입니다. 더 빠른 서비스를 원하시면 저희 웹사이트에서 온라인으로 주문하실 수 있습니다. 또한, 저희 웹사이트는 저희의 특별한 메뉴들에 대한 구체적인 세부정보를 제공합니다.

You are listening to →/ Radio Seven's entertainment and media report. ↘// Our first guest in this morning →/ is Simon Clark, →/ the producer of →/ the Oscar-winning documentary film →/ Night Mail. ↘// On today's show, →/ Mr. Clark will tell us about →/ his background, ↗/ experiences ↗/ in film making and his other projects. ↘// Now, →/ let's welcome Mr. Clark. ↘//

당신은 Radio Seven's entertainment and media report를 듣고 계십니다. 오늘 아침 첫 게스트는 다큐멘터리 부문 오스카 수상작 나이트 메일의 감독이신 사이먼 클라크입니다. 오늘의 쇼에서 클라크씨는 자신의 배경과 영화 제작 경험 그리고 그의 다른 작품들에 대해 얘기해 줄 것입니다. 이제 클라크씨를 환영합시다.

Question 3

장소	This picture was <u>taken at a library</u>.	이 사진은 도서관에서 찍힌 사진입니다.

인원	There are three women in this picture.	이 사진에는 3명의 여자들이 있습니다.

중심 대상	On the right, two of them are <u>standing at the information desk</u>, and they seem like college students.	오른쪽에는 그들 중 2명이 안내 데스크에서 서있는데 대학생 같아 보입니다.

주변 대상	In the background, I can see many books and bookshelves.	배경에는 많은 책들과 책장들이 있습니다.

상황	Overall, it seems like two students are <u>registering for something important</u>.	전반적으로 두 학생이 중요한 것을 등록하고 있는 것 같아 보입니다.

Question 4

장소	This picture was <u>taken at an outdoor market</u>.	이 사진은 야외 시장에서 찍힌 사진입니다.

인원	There are many people.	많은 사람들이 있습니다.

중심 대상	On the left, there is a man who is <u>carrying a plastic bag</u>. On the right, there are boxes, bags, and parasols.	왼쪽에는 한 남자가 비닐봉지를 들고 있습니다. 오른쪽에는 상자들, 장바구니들, 그리고 파라솔들이 있습니다.

주변 대상	In the background, I can see buildings and trees.	배경에는 건물들과 나무들이 보입니다.

상황	Overall, it seems like people are <u>enjoying shopping</u> at the outdoor market.	전반적으로 사람들은 야외 시장에서 장보는 것을 즐기고 있는 것 같습니다.

🔊 Imagine that the US marketing firm is conducting research about streaming services that you use to watch television shows.
A streaming service is a service that sends videos or music over the internet so that people can watch or listen to it immediately rather than having to download it.

미국 마케팅 회사가 텔레비전 쇼를 시청하기 위해 당신이 사용하는 스트리밍 서비스에 대해 연구를 수행하고 있다고 가정해보십시오. 스트리밍 서비스는 사람들이 동영상이나 음악을 다운받지 않고 인터넷을 통해 실시간으로 시청하거나 들을 수 있는 서비스입니다.

Question 5

Q How often do you stream television shows and what do you usually watch?

당신은 얼마나 자주 텔레비전 쇼를 스트리밍하고 주로 무엇을 시청하나요?

A I stream television shows almost every day and I usually watch American dramas. They are fun.

저는 거의 매일 텔레비전 쇼를 스트리밍하고 주로 미국 드라마를 봅니다.
이것들은 재미있습니다.

Question 6

Q When was the last time you streamed a television show and what service did you use?

마지막으로 텔레비전 쇼를 스트리밍 한 것이 언제이며, 어떤 서비스를 이용했나요?

A I last streamed a television show this morning and I used Netflix.
They offer tons of videos at low prices.

오늘 아침에 마지막으로 텔레비전 쇼를 스트리밍하였고 넷플릭스를 사용했습니다.
그들은 저렴한 가격에 많은 영상을 제공합니다.

Q When deciding which streaming service to use, which is a more influential factor in your decision-making: other viewers' reviews on the service or advertisements of the service?

서비스에 대한 다른 시청자들의 리뷰 또는 서비스에 대한 광고 중 어떤 스트리밍 서비스를 사용할지 결정할 때, 어떤 것이 당신의 의사 결정에 더 영향을 미치는 요소인가요?

`IM3-IH` When choosing a streaming service, I consider others' reviews more.
That's because users frankly talk about the pros and cons of the services. So, I can choose one that offers better services.
This is why.

스트리밍 서비스를 선택할 때, 저는 다른 사람들의 리뷰를 더 많이 고려합니다. 이용자들이 서비스의 장단점을 솔직하게 이야기하기 때문입니다. 그래서 저는 더 나은 서비스를 제공하는 것을 선택할 수 있습니다.
이것이 그 이유입니다.

`AL-AH` When choosing a streaming service, I consider others' reviews more.
That's because users frankly talk about the pros and cons of the services. Also, those reviews are based on their actual usage experience. So, I can figure out which company offers better services.
To sum up, I think viewers' reviews are reliable and trustworthy.
This is why.

스트리밍 서비스를 선택할 때, 저는 다른 사람들의 리뷰를 더 많이 고려합니다. 이용자들이 서비스의 장단점을 솔직하게 이야기하기 때문입니다. 또한 이러한 리뷰는 실제 사용 경험을 기반으로 합니다. 그래서 저는 어떤 회사가 더 나은 서비스를 제공하는지 알 수 있습니다.
요약하자면 시청자들의 후기는 믿을 만하고 신뢰할 수 있다고 생각합니다.
이것이 그 이유입니다.

Business Seminar for Small Businesses

[Global E-business Association] May 15, Wednesday, Leonardo Hall 203

9:00 A.M. - 10:00 A.M.	Welcome address	Jennifer Miller
10:00 A.M. - 11:00 A.M.	Introducing new approaches of market analysis	Lisa Henderson
11:00 A.M. - 12:00 P.M.	Lunch	-
12:00 P.M. - 1:00 P.M.	Lecture: time management and using resources	Wayne Xia
1:00 P.M. - 2:00 P.M.	Workshop: improving marketing strategies	Alan Callie
2:00 P.M. - 3:00 P.M.	Discussion: 5 steps of online market research (computer-based, laptops required)	Lisa Henderson
3:00 P.M. - 4:00 P.M.	Lecture: ways to think differently	Sue Chang

🔊 Hi, I heard that you will hold a business seminar for small business in May. Can I ask a few questions about the seminar?

안녕하세요, 5월에 Business Seminar for Small Businesses가 열린다고 들었습니다. 세미나에 대해 몇 가지 물어봐도 될까요?

Question 8

Q What is the date of the seminar and what time will it start?

세미나 날짜는 언제이며, 몇 시에 시작합니까?

A The date of the seminar is May 15th, Wednesday and it will start at 9 A.M.

세미나의 날짜는 5월 15일 수요일이며, 세미나는 오전 9시에 시작합니다.

Question 9

Q I heard that the seminar includes a session about improving marketing strategies. Will it be in the morning?

세미나에는 improving marketing strategies에 관한 세션이 포함되어 있다고 들었습니다. 아침에 열리는 세션입니까?

A No, the session about improving marketing strategies will be in the afternoon from 1 to 2 P.M.

아니요, improving marketing strategies에 관한 세션은 오후 1시부터 2시까지입니다.

Question 10

Q Last year, I was very impressed by Lisa Henderson's speech. Could you give me all the details of the sessions that Lisa Henderson will lead?

작년에 리사 헨더슨의 연설이 감명 깊었습니다. 리사 헨더슨이 진행하는 모든 세션에 대한 세부사항들을 알 수 있을까요?

A Sure, there are two. First, Lisa will introduce new approaches of market analysis from 10 to 11 A.M. Second, Lisa will lead a discussion on 5 steps of online market research from 2 to 3 P.M. It's a computer-based session and you should bring your laptop to attend it. That's all.

네, 두 개 있어요. 먼저 리사는 오전 10시부터 11시까지 시장 분석의 새로운 접근법을 소개할 것입니다. 두 번째로는 리사는 오후 2시부터 3시까지 온라인 시장 조사의 5단계에 대한 토론을 진행할 것입니다. 컴퓨터로 진행되는 세션이라 노트북을 가지고 오셔야 합니다. 이상입니다.

🔊 Which of the following would contribute the MOST to living a satisfying life? Give causes or examples to support your opinion.

- Having a nice job
- Exercising regularly
- Spending time with loved ones

다음 중 만족스러운 삶을 사는데 가장 기여하는 것은 무엇입니까? 당신의 의견을 뒷받침할 이유나 예를 제시하세요.

- 좋은 직업을 가지기
- 규칙적으로 운동하기
- 사랑하는 사람들과 즐거운 시간 보내기

IM3

I think having a nice job would contribute most to living a satisfying life. I have two reasons for this.

First, people feel happy when they do something they like. Working from Monday to Friday every week is a huge portion of our life. So, having a nice job is important for one's happiness.

Second, if I have a great job that pays me well, I can enjoy more things in life. I don't need to worry about costly living expenses.

These are the reasons.

저는 좋은 직업을 갖는 것이 만족스러운 삶을 사는 데 가장 기여한다고 생각합니다.
이에 대한 두 가지 이유가 있습니다.

첫째, 사람들은 그들이 좋아하는 일을 할 때 행복을 느낍니다. 매주 월요일부터 금요일까지 일하는 것은 우리 삶의 큰 부분입니다. 그래서 좋은 직업을 갖는 것은 사람의 행복에 중요합니다.

둘째, 만약 제가 돈을 잘 버는 멋진 직업을 가지고 있다면, 제 인생에서 더 많은 것을 즐길 수 있습니다. 고가의 생활비에 대해 걱정할 필요가 없습니다.

이것들이 이유입니다.

IH

I think having a nice job would contribute the most to living a satisfying life. I have two reasons for this.

First, people feel happy when they do something they like. Working from Monday to Friday every week is a huge portion of our life. So, the level of job satisfaction significantly influences one's happiness.

Second, if I have a great job that pays me well, I can enjoy more things in life. Also, I don't need to worry about costly living expenses. As a result, I can live a stable life.

These are the reasons.

저는 좋은 직업을 갖는 것이 만족스러운 삶을 사는 데 가장 기여한다고 생각합니다.
이에 대한 두 가지 이유가 있습니다.

첫째, 사람들은 그들이 좋아하는 일을 할 때 행복을 느낍니다. 매주 월요일부터 금요일까지 일하는 것은 우리 삶의 큰 부분입니다. 그래서, 직무 만족도의 수준은 행복에 상당히 영향을 미칩니다.

둘째, 만약 제가 돈을 잘 버는 멋진 직업을 가지고 있다면, 제 인생에서 더 많은 것을 즐길 수 있습니다. 또한, 고가의 생활비에 대해 걱정할 필요가 없습니다. 결과적으로, 저는 안정적인 삶을 살 수 있습니다.

이것들이 이유입니다.

AL-AH

I think having a nice job would contribute the most to living a satisfying life. I have two reasons for this.

First, people feel happy when they do something they like. Most people spend 8 hours a day from Monday to Friday, and it's a huge portion of our life. So, the level of job satisfaction significantly influences one's happiness.

Second, if I have a great job that pays me well, I can enjoy more things in life. For example, I can buy a nicer car, a bigger house, and other goods for life. Also, I don't need to worry about costly living expenses. As a result, I can live a stable life.

These are the reasons.

저는 좋은 직업을 갖는 것이 만족스러운 삶을 사는 데 가장 기여한다고 생각합니다.
이에 대한 두 가지 이유가 있습니다.

첫째, 사람들은 그들이 좋아하는 일을 할 때 행복을 느낍니다. 대부분의 사람들은 월요일부터 금요일까지 하루에 8시간을 보내는 데 이것은 우리 삶의 상당 부분을 차지합니다. 그래서 직무 만족도의 수준은 행복에 상당한 영향을 미칩니다.

둘째, 만약 제가 돈을 잘 버는 멋진 직업을 가지고 있다면, 제 인생에서 더 많은 것을 즐길 수 있습니다. 예를 들어, 저는 더 좋은 차, 더 큰 집, 그리고 다른 물건들을 평생 살 수 있습니다. 또한, 고가의 생활비에 대해 걱정할 필요가 없습니다. 결과적으로, 저는 안정적인 삶을 살 수 있습니다.

이것들이 이유입니다.

03 실전유형 모의고사

모범답변·템플릿

Question 1

Hello and welcome to →/ Everson music podcast. ↘// Today, →/ I am joined by Gabriel Fletcher, →/ an assistant professor →/ at Central University. ↘// We'll be discussing →/ some of the greatest albums →/ of the past year. ↘// We'll start by reviewing →/ my favorite pop, ↗/ classical, ↗/ and jazz artists. ↘//

안녕하십니까. Everson 음악 팟캐스트에 오신 것을 환영합니다. 오늘, 저는 센트럴 대학의 조교수인 Gabriel Fletcher 와 함께하고 있습니다. 우리는 지난 해 최고의 앨범들 중 몇 가지에 대해 논의할 예정입니다. 우선 제가 좋아하는 팝, 클래식, 재즈 아티스트들을 살펴보는 것으로 시작하겠습니다.

Question 2

Thank you for →/ volunteering today →/ at our Art museum's Family Day. ↘// You are going to be →/ supporting our staff →/ in a variety of ways. ↘// To begin, →/ please report to the reception desk. ↘// You will get →/ your information form, ↗/ your museum badge, ↗/ and a voucher for the cafeteria. ↘// If you need help →/ finding anything, →/ please ask one of our staffs. ↘//

저희 미술관의 가족의 날을 위해 자원봉사를 지원해 주셔서 감사합니다. 여러분은 다양한 방법으로 저희 직원들을 도와드릴 겁니다. 우선, 접수처를 방문해주시면 안내서와 박물관 배지, 그리고 구내식당 이용권을 받으실 것입니다. 무엇이든 찾으시는 데 도움이 필요하시면 저희 직원에게 물어보세요.

장소	This picture was taken in a conference room.	이 사진은 회의실에서 찍혔습니다.

인원	There are six people having a meeting.	이 장면에는 6명의 사람들이 회의하고 있습니다.

중심 대상	In the center, two of them are giving a presentation in front of an easel, and the others are listening.	중앙에는 그들 중 두 명이 칠판대 앞에서 발표를 하고 있고, 다른 사람들은 듣고 있습니다.

주변 대상	In the background, there is a huge window.	배경에는 커다란 창문이 있습니다.

상황	Overall, it seems like they are discussing something important.	전반적으로 그들은 중요한 것을 논의하고 있는 것 같습니다.

장소	This picture was <u>taken at a cafe</u>.	이 사진은 카페에서 찍힌 사진입니다.
인원	There are many people.	많은 사람들이 있습니다.
중심 대상	In the foreground, there are two men <u>chatting together</u>. They are sitting on a sofa.	앞쪽에는 두 남자가 함께 얘기하고 있습니다. 그들은 소파에 앉아 있습니다.
주변 대상	In the background, there are three people, and two of them on the right are <u>putting food onto their plates</u>.	배경에는 세 사람이 있고, 오른쪽에 있는 두 사람은 접시에 음식을 담고 있습니다.
상황	Overall, it seems like people are <u>socializing at the cafe</u>.	전반적으로 사람들은 카페에서 어울리고 있는 것 같습니다.

🔊 Imagine that World Vision Company is conducting research in your area. You have agreed to participate in a telephone interview about donating money for organizations.

World Vision Company가 당신의 지역에서 연구를 수행하고 있다고 가정해 보십시오. 당신은 단체에 기부하는 것에 대한 전화 인터뷰에 참여하기로 동의했습니다.

Question 5

Q Do you think it is a good idea for charities or organizations to ask people to donate money on the radio? Why or why not?

자선단체나 기관들이 라디오를 통해 사람들에게 돈을 기부하라고 부탁하는 것이 좋은 생각이라고 생각하나요? 이유는 무엇입니까?

A No, I don't think it is a good idea because not many people listen to the radio these days.

저는 좋은 아이디어가 아니라고 생각합니다. 왜냐하면 요즘 라디오를 듣는 사람들이 많지 않기 때문입니다.

Question 6

Q Do you ever use a mobile phone to donate your money? Why or why not?

당신은 핸드폰을 사용해서 기부한 적이 있나요? 이유는 무엇입니까?

A No, I have never donated money using a mobile phone because I've never had a chance to do so.

아니요. 저는 한번도 핸드폰을 사용해서 돈을 기부한 적이 없습니다. 왜냐하면 그렇게 할 기회가 없었기 때문입니다.

Q Which of the following organizations would you be willing to donate to, and why?

- An environmental organization
- An organization that does medical research
- An educational organization

다음 중 어느 단체에 기부할 의향이 있으며, 그 이유는 무엇입니까?

- 환경단체
- 의료 연구를 수행하는 기관
- 교육기관

IM3-IH I would donate money to an organization that does medical research, and here is why.
These days, pandemics are a great threat to the entire human race. Although many organizations try their best, they still need financial aid.
This is why.

저는 의학 연구를 하는 단체에 돈을 기부할 것이고, 여기 그 이유가 있습니다.
요즘 유행병은 인류 전체에 큰 위협이 되고 있습니다. 비록 많은 단체들이 최선을 다하지만, 그들은 여전히 재정적인 지원이 필요합니다.
이것이 그 이유입니다.

AL-AH I would donate money to an organization that does medical research, and here is why.
These days, pandemics are a great threat to the entire human race. Although many organizations try their best to make vaccines and medicines right after an outbreak, they still face many challenges in meeting people's needs.
Considering this, donations will help them to deal with financial problems.
This is why.

저는 의학 연구를 하는 단체에 돈을 기부할 것이고, 여기 그 이유가 있습니다.
요즘 유행병은 인류 전체에 큰 위협이 되고 있습니다. 비록 많은 단체들이 발병 직후 백신과 의약품을 만들기 위해 최선을 다하지만, 그들은 여전히 사람들의 요구를 충족시키는 데 많은 어려움을 겪고 있습니다.
이러한 점을 고려할 때 기부는 그들이 재정적인 문제를 해결하는 데 도움이 될 것입니다.
이것이 그 이유입니다.

Schedule on February 4

Richard McDonald / Executive director, Interesting Corporation

9:00 - 11:00 A.M.	Conference call (CEO, Dellie food)
11:00 A.M. - Noon	Meeting (Donald Fella, manager, financial department)
Noon - 1:00 P.M.	Presentation (new employees, R&R)
1:00 - 2:00 P.M.	~~Lunch with Marta Jones~~ *moved to March 5, 4 P.M.*
2:00 - 3:00 P.M.	Online communication with Applicants
3:00 - 4:00 P.M.	Meeting (Marie Darren, manager, marketing department)
4:00 - 5:00 P.M.	Review, sales performance (director, sales department)

🔊 Hi, I am Richard McDonald and let me ask questions about my schedule on February 4th.

안녕하세요, 저는 Richard McDonald이고 2월 4일 제 일정에 대해 물어볼 게 있습니다.

Question 8

Q I need to leave early tomorrow. What is the last item of tomorrow's schedule and what time does it end?

저는 내일 일찍 떠나야 합니다. 내일 일정의 마지막 일정은 무엇이고, 몇 시에 끝납니까?

A Your last schedule tomorrow is reviewing the sales performance with the sales department director and it will end at 5 P.M.

내일 당신의 마지막 일정은 영업부장과 영업 실적을 검토하는 것이고 오후 5시에 끝날 예정입니다.

Question 9

Q I remember that I will have lunch with Marta Jones tomorrow. Could you confirm that schedule?

내일 Marta Jones와 점심 먹을 예정이라고 기억하고 있습니다. 그 일정을 확인해 주시겠습니까?

A Actually, your lunch appointment with Marta has been moved to March 5th at 4 P.M.

실은, Marta와의 점심 약속이 3월 5일 오후 4시로 변경되었습니다.

Question 10

Q Please give me all the information of meetings tomorrow.

내일 회의에 관한 모든 정보를 주세요.

A Sure, there are two meetings tomorrow.
First, you will have a meeting with the financial department manager Donald Fella from 11 A.M. to noon.
Second, you will have a meeting with the marketing department manager Marie Darren from 3 to 4 P.M.

물론이죠. 내일 두 개의 회의가 있습니다. 첫 번째, 오전 11시부터 정오까지 재무부 관리자 Donald Fella와 회의가 있을 예정입니다. 두 번째로 오후 3시부터 4시까지 마케팅 부서장 Marie Darren과 회의가 있을 예정입니다.

🔊 Do you agree or disagree with the following statement?
"A person's job satisfaction is affected more by salary than the assigned duties."

다음 명제에 동의하십니까, 동의하지 않으십니까?
"한 사람의 직무 만족도는 할당된 직무보다 급여에 의해 더 영향을 받습니다."

IM3 I agree that a person's job satisfaction is influenced more by salary than the assigned duties. There are two reasons for this.

First, a high salary will increase the quality of my life. I can enjoy more things in my personal life. This will make me satisfied.

Second, a high-paying job will give me a sense of fulfillment. That's because good pay means that I get valued and respected by the company.

These are my reasons.

저는 한 사람의 직업 만족도가 할당된 임무보다 급여에 더 많이 영향을 받는다는 것에 동의합니다. 여기에는 두 가지 이유가 있습니다.

첫째, 높은 연봉은 제 삶의 질을 높일 것입니다. 높은 급여로, 저는 제 개인 삶에서 더 많은 것들을 누릴 수 있습니다. 이것은 저를 만족시킬 것입니다.

둘째, 높은 보수를 받는 직업은 저에게 성취감을 줄 것입니다. 좋은 보수는 제가 일하는 회사로부터 가치를 인정받고 존중을 받는 것을 의미하기 때문입니다.

이것들이 제 이유입니다.

IH I agree that a person's job satisfaction is influenced more by salary than the assigned duties. There are two reasons for this.

First, a high salary will increase the quality of my life. With a high salary, I can enjoy more things in my personal life. This will make me satisfied.

Second, a high-paying job will give me a sense of fulfillment. That's because good pay means that I get valued and respected by the company that I work for. Therefore, I will feel rewarded for what I do at the workplace.

These are my reasons.

저는 한 사람의 직업 만족도가 할당된 임무보다 급여에 더 많이 영향을 받는다는 것에 동의합니다. 여기에는 두 가지 이유가 있습니다.

첫째, 높은 연봉은 제 삶의 질을 높일 것입니다. 높은 급여로, 저는 제 개인 삶에서 더 많은 것들을 누릴 수 있습니다. 이것은 저를 만족시킬 것입니다.

둘째, 높은 보수를 받는 직업은 저에게 성취감을 줄 것입니다. 좋은 보수는 제가 일하는 회사로부터 가치를 인정받고 존중을 받는 것을 의미하기 때문입니다. 그러므로, 저는 직장에서 제가 하는 일에 대해 보람을 느낄 것입니다.

이것들이 제 이유입니다.

AL-AH I agree that a person's job satisfaction is influenced more by salary than the assigned duties. There are two reasons for this.

First, a high salary will increase the quality of my life. For example, I can afford a bigger house or a fancier car, and I can also enjoy more things in my personal life. This will make me more content with my job.

Second, a high-paying job will give me a sense of fulfillment. That's because good pay means that I get valued and respected by the company that I work for. Therefore, I will feel rewarded for what I do at the workplace, and it will help me build a healthy ego.

These are my reasons.

저는 한 사람의 직업 만족도가 할당된 임무보다 급여에 더 많이 영향을 받는다는 것에 동의합니다. 여기에는 두 가지 이유가 있습니다.

첫째, 높은 연봉은 제 삶의 질을 높일 것입니다. 예를 들어, 저는 더 큰 집이나 더 멋진 차를 살 수 있고 제 개인 삶에서 더 많은 것들을 누릴 수 있습니다. 이것은 제가 제 일에 더 만족하게 만들 것입니다.

둘째, 높은 보수를 받는 직업은 저에게 성취감을 줄 것입니다. 좋은 보수는 제가 일하는 회사로부터 가치를 인정받고 존중을 받는 것을 의미하기 때문입니다. 그러므로, 저는 직장에서 제가 하는 일에 대해 보람을 느낄 것이고 이는 제가 자존감을 높이도록 도와 줄 것입니다.

이것들이 제 이유입니다.

04 실전유형 모의고사

모범답변·템플릿

Question 1

If you are not getting →/ the cell phone service you want, →/ consider switching →/ to Johnson mobile. ↘// Our service is faster, ↗/ more reliable ↗/ and more affordable →/ than anything ↗/ you'll find on the market. ↘// And we are providing a free service →/ for three weeks →/ to new customers. ↘// So, call us now. ↘//

만약 당신이 원하는 휴대폰 서비스를 받지 못했다면, Johnson mobile로 바꾸는 것을 고려해 보세요. 저희 서비스는 시중에 나와있는 어떤 서비스보다 더 빠르고, 안정적이고, 저렴합니다. 그리고 우리는 신규 고객에게 3주간 무료 서비스를 제공하고 있습니다. 그러니 지금 전화 주세요.

Question 2

Hello, →/ and welcome to the seminar →/ on social media for business. ↘// This seminar is to help you →/ enhance marketing strategies →/ of your business sales, ↗/ brand awareness ↗/ and customer loyalty. ↘// Social media, →/ a powerful marketing tool, →/ can help you →/ achieve these goals. ↘// As a first step, →/ we will provide you →/ essential tips and advice →/ to use popular apps →/ in an effective way →/ to make customers →/ interested in your services. ↘//

안녕하세요, 비즈니스를 위한 소셜 미디어 세미나에 오신 것을 환영합니다. 이번 세미나는 귀사의 판매, 브랜드 인지도, 그리고 고객 충성도에 관한 마케팅 전략을 강화하는 데 도움이 됩니다. 강력한 마케팅 도구인 소셜 미디어는 이러한 목표를 달성하는 데 도움을 줄 수 있습니다. 첫 번째 단계로, 저희는 고객들이 귀사의 서비스에 관심을 가질 수 있도록 효과적인 방법으로 인기 있는 앱을 사용할 수 있는 매우 중요한 팁을 제공할 것입니다.

Question 3

장소	This picture was <u>taken at a hotel</u>.	이 사진은 호텔에서 찍혔습니다.
인원	There are three people in this scene.	이 장면에는 세 명의 사람들이 있습니다.
중심 대상	In the center, a young couple is <u>standing at the reception</u>. On the left, an employee is <u>pointing at a paper</u> and <u>explaining something</u>.	중앙에는 젊은 커플이 리셉션에 서있습니다. 왼쪽에는, 한 직원이 종이를 가리키며 무언가를 설명하고 있습니다.
주변 대상	In the background, I can see chairs, plants, and small windows.	배경에는 의자, 식물, 그리고 작은 창문들이 보입니다.
상황	Overall, it seems like <u>those customers are filling out a form</u>.	전반적으로 그들은 양식을 작성하고 있는 것 같습니다.

34

장소	This picture was taken at the front desk of a hotel.	이 사진은 호텔 프런트에서 찍힌 사진입니다.

인원	There are three people in the picture.	사진 속에는 세 사람이 있습니다.

중심 대상	On the left, the receptionist is on standby, and the man on the right is serving the customer.	왼쪽은 접수계원이 대기 중이고, 오른쪽 남자는 손님 접대를 하고 있습니다.

주변 대상	In the background, there are many decorations, like a painting.	배경에는 그림과 같은 여러가지 장식이 있습니다.

상황	Overall, it seems like the woman is checking in at the hotel.	전반적으로 여자가 호텔에 체크인하는 것 같습니다.

🔊 Imagine a marketing firm is conducting research in your community. You have agreed to participate in a telephone interview about birthday gifts.

한 마케팅 회사가 당신의 지역에서 연구를 수행하고 있다고 가정해 보십시오. 당신은 생일 선물에 관한 전화 인터뷰에 참여하기로 동의했습니다.

Question 5

Q When was the last time you gave a birthday gift, and who was it for?

마지막으로 생일 선물을 준 게 언제이며, 누굴 위한 것이었습니까?

A The last time I gave a birthday gift was two years ago and it was for my best friend.

마지막으로 생일 선물 준 것은 2년 전이고 저의 절친을 위한 것이었습니다.

Question 6

Q Which makes a better birthday gift: money or a present from a store, and why?

돈과 매장에서 산 선물 중 어떤 것이 더 좋은 생일 선물입니까? 이유는 무엇입니까?

A I think money is a better gift because it's more practical. I mean, we can buy exactly what we want with cash.

저는 돈이 더 좋은 선물이라고 생각합니다. 왜냐하면 더 실용적이기 때문입니다. 즉, 현금으로 원하는 것을 살 수 있습니다.

Q Many couples these days make a list of birthday gifts that they want to receive and exchange it with each other. Do you think it is a good idea for them to do this? Why or why not?

요즘 많은 커플들은 그들이 받고 싶은 생일 선물 목록을 만들고 그것을 서로 교환합니다. 여러분은 그들이 이것을 하는 것이 좋은 생각이라고 생각하나요? 그 이유는 무엇인가요?

IM3-IH Yes, I think it is a good idea for couples to share a wish list for birthday gifts.
That is because they don't need to think a lot about what to buy.
Also, there is no disappointment because they can expect what to get.
This is why.

네, 저는 커플들이 생일 선물로 위시리스트를 공유하는 것이 좋은 생각인 것 같습니다. 그것은 그들이 무엇을 살지에 대해 많이 생각할 필요가 없기 때문입니다. 또한 그들은 무엇을 얻을지 기대할 수 있기 때문에 실망감이 없습니다. 이것이 그 이유입니다.

AL-AH Yes, I think it is a good idea for couples to share a wish list for birthday gifts.
That is because they don't need to think a lot about what to buy. It will save them time and energy when choosing a gift.
Also, there is less chance of disappointment after receiving a present because they can expect what to get. So, I think it's a safe choice.
This is why.

네, 저는 커플들이 생일 선물로 위시리스트를 공유하는 것이 좋은 생각인 것 같습니다. 그것은 그들이 무엇을 살지에 대해 많이 생각할 필요가 없기 때문입니다. 그것은 그들이 선물을 고를 때 시간과 에너지를 절약할 것입니다. 또한 그들은 무엇을 받을지 기대할 수 있기 때문에 선물을 받은 후에 실망할 가능성이 적습니다. 그래서 저는 안전한 선택이라고 생각합니다. 이것이 그 이유입니다.

Conference of food scientists
Rayon hotel, Tony ballroom

September 21, Thursday	9:00 – 10:00 A.M.	Registration (hotel lobby)
	10:00 – 11:00 A.M.	Presentation: boosting nutrition through food science (Jack Nicole)
	11:00 A.M. - Noon	Workshop: updates on global food standards (Lora Kimberly)
	Noon – 1:00 P.M.	Discussion: meals for children under 9
September 22, Friday	9:00 – 10:00 A.M.	Breakfast (Tillet dining hall)
	10:00 – 11:00 A.M.	Workshop: a closer look at food preservation (Jason Molina)
	11:00 A.M. - Noon	Lecture: how to choose the right ingredients for the elderly (Bobby Lim)
	Noon – 1:00 P.M.	Closing remarks

🔊 Hi, I am very interested in your conference in September. Can I ask a few questions about it schedule?

안녕하세요, 저는 9월에 열리는 컨퍼런스에 관심이 많습니다. 이 일정에 대해 몇 가지 질문해도 될까요?

Question 8

Q What time will the first presentation start on Thursday, and what is it called?

목요일에 진행되는 첫 번째 발표는 언제 시작되며, 무엇입니까?

A The first presentation on Thursday will start at 10 A.M. and it is about boosting nutrition through food science.

목요일에 진행되는 첫 번째 발표는 오전 10시에 시작하고 이것은 boosting nutrition through food science에 관한 것입니다.

Q The conference will be held in Mayfair hotel, right?

이 컨퍼런스는 Mayfair 호텔에서 열릴 예정인 것이 맞나요?

A No, I am afraid you have the wrong information. The conference will be held at the Tony ballroom of Rayon hotel.

아닙니다. 당신은 잘못된 정보를 가지고 계신 것 같습니다. 이 컨퍼런스는 Rayon hotel의 Tony ballroom에서 열릴 예정입니다.

Q I am very interested in workshops. Could you give me all the details of the workshops?

저는 워크숍에 관심이 많습니다. 워크숍의 모든 세부사항을 알려주시겠습니까?

A Sure, we have two workshops. The first one will be on September 21st from 11 A.M. to noon. It's about updates on global food standards and it will be led by Lora Kimberly. And the second workshop will be on September 22nd from 10 to 11 A.M. It's about a closer look at food preservation and it will be led by Jason Molina. That's all.

물론이죠. 두 개의 워크숍이 있습니다. 첫 번째는 9월 21일 오전 11시부터 정오까지 열릴 예정입니다. 이것은 updates on global found standards에 관한 것이고 Lora Kimberly가 진행할 예정입니다. 그리고, 두 번째 워크숍은 9월 22일 오전 10시부터 11시까지 열릴 예정입니다. 이것은 a closer look at food preservation에 관한 것이고 Jason Molina가 진행할 예정입니다. 이상입니다.

Question 11

🔊 Which do you think contributes more to a team's effectiveness: having an experienced leader or having a good relationship among team members?

경험이 풍부한 리더와 팀원들 간의 좋은 관계 중 어느 것이 팀의 효율성에 더 기여한다고 생각하십니까?

IM3 I think having a good relationship among team members contributes more to a team's effectiveness than having an experienced leader. There are two reasons for this.

First, it will promote effective communication. For example, they would communicate with an open mind.

Second, it creates a positive atmosphere. This will help them be more creative and productive.

These are the reasons why I think in this way.

저는 경험이 풍부한 리더가 있는 것보다 팀원들 간의 좋은 관계가 팀의 효율성에 더 기여한다고 생각합니다. 여기에는 두 가지 이유가 있습니다.

첫째, 효과적인 의사소통을 촉진할 것입니다. 예를 들어, 그들은 열린 마음으로 의사소통을 할 것입니다.

둘째, 긍정적인 분위기를 만들어 줍니다. 이것은 그들이 더 창의적이고 생산적이 되도록 도울 것입니다.

이것들이 제가 이렇게 생각하는 이유입니다.

IH I think having a good relationship among team members contributes more to a team's effectiveness than having an experienced leader. There are two reasons for this.

First, it will promote effective communication. For example, when team members get along well, they tend to communicate with an open mind.

Second, it creates a positive atmosphere. A pleasant mood encourages team members to work with a more positive mindset. This will help them be more creative and productive.

These are the reasons why I think in this way.

저는 경험이 풍부한 리더가 있는 것보다 팀원들 간의 좋은 관계가 팀의 효율성에 더 기여한다고 생각합니다. 여기에는 두 가지 이유가 있습니다.

첫째, 효과적인 의사소통을 촉진할 것입니다. 예를 들어, 팀원들이 잘 지낼 때, 그들은 열린 마음으로 소통하는 경향이 있습니다.

둘째, 긍정적인 분위기를 만들어 줍니다. 유쾌한 기분은 팀원들이 더 긍정적인 사고방식으로 일하도록 격려합니다. 이것은 그들이 더 창의적이고 생산적이 되도록 도울 것입니다.

이것들이 제가 이렇게 생각하는 이유입니다.

AL-AH I think having a good relationship among team members contributes more to a team's effectiveness than having an experienced leader. There are two reasons for this.

First, it will promote effective communication. For example, when team members get along well, they tend to communicate with an open mind. And this honest communication helps them understand each other's perspectives and ideas, which brings better achievements.

Second, it creates a positive atmosphere. A pleasant mood encourages team members to work with a more positive mindset. This will help them be more creative and productive. Also, a positive team spirit will reduce conflicts among teammates.

These are the reasons why I think in this way.

저는 경험이 풍부한 리더가 있는 것보다 팀원들 간의 좋은 관계가 팀의 효율성에 더 기여한다고 생각합니다. 여기에는 두 가지 이유가 있습니다.

첫째, 효과적인 의사소통을 촉진할 것입니다. 예를 들어, 팀원들이 잘 지낼 때, 그들은 열린 마음으로 소통하는 경향이 있습니다. 그리고 이러한 솔직한 의사소통은 그들이 서로의 관점과 생각을 이해하는 데 도움이 되고, 이것은 더 나은 성과를 가져옵니다.

둘째, 긍정적인 분위기를 만들어 줍니다. 유쾌한 기분은 팀원들이 더 긍정적인 사고방식으로 일하도록 격려합니다. 이것은 그들이 더 창의적이고 생산적이 되도록 도울 것입니다. 또한, 긍정적인 팀 정신은 팀 동료들 사이의 갈등을 줄여줄 것입니다.

이것들이 제가 이렇게 생각하는 이유입니다.

05

실전유형 모의고사

모범답변·템플릿

Question 1

Good morning, →/ College Radio listeners. ↘// In weather forecast, →/ today is supposed to be →/ a beautiful sunny day. ↘// It's a great day →/ to study outdoors, ↗/ go to a coffee shop, ↗/ or walk in the park. ↘// We anticipate →/ a moderate breeze, →/ which will make →/ pleasant winds →/ while in the sunshine. ↘//

좋은 아침입니다 College Radio 청취자 여러분. 일기예보에 따르면 오늘은 화창한 날이 될 것 같습니다. 야외에서 공부하거나, 카페에 가거나, 공원을 산책하기에 좋은 날입니다. 햇살을 받으며 기분 좋은 바람을 느낄 수 있는 적당한 산들바람이 예상됩니다.

Question 2

Thank you for inviting me to speak at →/ this month's →/ Medical Care Conference. ↘// Before I begin my speech, →/ let me provide →/ a brief interview. ↘// In the past year, →/ I conducted →/ hundreds of interviews →/ with doctors, ↗/ patients ↗/ and other hospital staffs. ↘// I will be sharing a few things →/ I noticed about →/ how hospitals can provide →/ the best medical treatment →/ to their patients. ↘//

이번 달 Medical Care 회의에 저를 초청해 주셔서 감사합니다. 연설을 시작하기 전에 간단한 인터뷰 내용을 제공하겠습니다. 지난 한 해 동안, 저는 의사, 환자, 그리고 다른 병원 직원들과 수백 번의 인터뷰를 진행했습니다. 병원이 환자들에게 최고의 진료를 제공할 수 있는 방법에 대해 몇 가지 공유해 드리겠습니다.

Question 3

장소	This picture was <u>taken on the street</u>.	이 사진은 거리에서 찍혔습니다.
인원	There are several people in this picture.	이 사진에는 여러 사람들이 있습니다.
중심 대상	On the right, a man is <u>riding a bicycle</u>. Next to him, a woman is <u>waiting at a stoplight</u> with her daughter.	오른쪽에는, 한 남자가 자전거를 타고 있습니다. 남자 옆에는 한 여자가 딸과 함께 신호를 기다리고 있습니다.
주변 대상	In the background, there are trees <u>planted in a row</u>, and many cars are <u>parked along the street</u>.	배경에는 가로수가 줄지어 심어져 있고, 길을 따라 많은 차들이 주차되어 있습니다.
상황	Overall, it seems <u>peaceful and relaxing</u>.	전체적으로 평화롭고 여유로워 보입니다.

Question 4

장소	This picture was <u>taken at a lecture hall</u>.	이 사진은 강당에서 찍힌 사진입니다.
인원	There are many students and a professor in the picture.	사진 속에는 많은 학생들과 교수님이 있습니다.
중심 대상	At the front of the lecture hall, the professor is <u>giving a lecture</u>. Because the lecture hall is too large, the professor is <u>using a microphone</u>.	강의실 앞에서 교수님이 강의를 하고 있습니다. 강의실이 너무 넓어서 교수님이 마이크를 사용하고 계십니다.
주변 대상	On the left, there are two <u>enormous projector screens</u>.	왼쪽에는 두 개의 큰 프로젝터 스크린이 있습니다.
상황	Overall, it seems like they are <u>in class</u>.	전반적으로 그들은 수업 중인 것 같습니다.

🔊 Imagine a newspaper company is conducting research in your area about listening to an audio podcast. A podcast is an episodic series of digital audio files that a user can download to a personal device to listen. You have agreed to participate in a telephone interview about your listening habits.

한 신문 회사가 당신의 지역에서 오디오 팟캐스트를 듣는 것에 대한 연구를 시행하고 있다고 가정해 보십시오. 팟캐스트는 디지털 오디오 파일의 에피소드 시리즈로 사용자가 개인 기기에 다운로드 할 수 있습니다. 당신은 당신의 청취 습관에 대한 전화 인터뷰에 참여하기로 동의하셨습니다.

Question 5

Q When was the last time you listened to an audio podcast, and what was it about?

마지막으로 오디오 팟캐스트를 들은 적이 언제이며 무엇에 관한 것이었나요?

A The last time I listened to a podcast was yesterday, and it was about healthy diet.

마지막으로 팟캐스트를 들은 것은 어제이며 건강한 식습관에 대한 것이었습니다.

Question 6

Q Would you listen to a podcast when taking a train or bus? Why or why not?

버스나 지하철을 탈 때 팟캐스트를 들으시겠어요? 이유는 무엇입니까?

A Yes, I would because it's fun and informative. Also, unlike watching YouTube videos or reading a book, it doesn't get me carsick.

네, 재미있고 유익하기 때문에 팟캐스트를 들을 겁니다. 또한, 유튜브 비디오나 책을 읽는 것과 다르게 차 멀미를 안 합니다.

Q What are the advantages of listening to an audio podcast instead of reading a book?

책을 읽는 대신 오디오 팟캐스트를 듣는 것의 장점은 무엇입니까?

IM3-IH There are some advantages of listening to an audio podcast instead of reading a book.

First, I can multitask because I can listen to it while doing other tasks.

Second, it's accessible anytime, anywhere.

This is why.

책을 읽는 것에 비해 오디오 팟캐스트를 듣는 것에는 몇 가지 장점이 있습니다.

첫째, 다른 작업을 하면서 들을 수 있기 때문에 멀티태스킹을 할 수 있습니다.

둘째, 언제 어디서나 들을 수 있습니다.

이것이 그 이유입니다.

AL-AH There are some advantages of listening to an audio podcast instead of reading a book.

First, I can multitask. For example, I can listen to an audio podcast while doing other tasks like driving, exercising, or cooking.

Second, it's more accessible. As far as I have a mobile device, I can listen to it anytime, anywhere.

This is why.

책을 읽는 것에 비해 오디오 팟캐스트를 듣는 것에는 몇 가지 장점이 있습니다.

첫째, 멀티태스킹을 할 수 있습니다. 예를 들어, 운전, 운동 또는 요리와 같은 다른 작업을 하면서 오디오 팟캐스트를 들을 수 있습니다.

둘째, 접근성이 더 좋습니다. 저는 모바일 기기만 있으면 언제 어디서나 들을 수 있습니다.

이것이 그 이유입니다.

LulkerBe Nature Park Running Trail
Open daily, May through November, 9 A.M. – 7 P.M.

Trail	Challenge	Distance	Note
Nathan peak	Difficult	10 kilometers	Stiff hills
Lone trail	Difficult	8 kilometers	
Wilson road	Difficult	9 kilometers	Cross bike trail
Tomato trail	Easy	2 kilometers	
Breeze rail	Intermediate	4 kilometers	
Wecantte Neva	Easy	1 kilometer	Designed for beginners

Ages 15 or younger should be accompanied by an adult

🔊 Let me ask you about the details about LulkerBe Nature Park Running Trail.

LulkerBe Nature Park Running Trail에 대한 자세한 정보에 대해 질문 하겠습니다.

Question 8

Q What days can I use your trails and what is the earliest time that I can run on your trails?

산책로를 이용할 수 있는 날은 언제이며, 산책로를 이용할 수 있는 가장 이른 시간대가 언제 입니까?

A We open every day from May to November and the earliest time you can use our trail is 9 A.M.

저희는 5월부터 11월까지 매일 열고, 저희 산책로를 이용할 수 있는 가장 이른 시간대는 오전 9시입니다.

Q My son wants to use one of your trails by himself. Is that ok?

제 아들이 산책로들 중 하나를 혼자서 이용하기를 원합니다. 괜찮습니까?

A It depends on how old he is. If he is 15 or younger, he should come with an adult. But if he is older than 15, he can use the trail alone.

아드님의 나이에 따라 달라집니다. 15세 이하라면 어른과 동행해야 하지만, 15살보다 나이가 많다면 혼자 산책로를 이용할 수 있습니다.

Question 10

Q I am an experienced runner for more than 10 years. Please give me all the details of trails that are suitable for experienced runners like me.

저는 10년 이상의 경험을 가지고 있는 달리기 선수입니다. 저처럼 노련한 달리기 선수들에게 적합한 산책로의 모든 세부사항을 알려주세요.

A Sure, we have three trails that are suitable for experienced runners like you. The first one is Nathan peak and it's 10 km long. Also, please be aware that it has quite stiff hills. The second one is Lone trail which is 8 km long. The last one is Wilson Road and it's 9 km long. Also, it has a cross bike trail. That's all.

물론이죠, 당신 같이 경험 많은 선수들에게 적합한 산책로가 3개 있습니다. 첫 번째는 Nathan peak이고 길이는 10km입니다. 또한, 언덕이 꽤 가파르다는 점 인지해 주세요. 두 번째는 8km 길이의 Lone trail입니다. 마지막은 Wilson road이고 길이는 9km입니다. 이곳에는 자전거 횡단로가 있습니다. 이상입니다.

🔊 Do you agree or disagree with the following statement?
"Employees should be permitted to use social networking sites to communicate with their colleagues in the workplace."

다음 명제에 동의하십니까, 동의하지 않으십니까?
"직원들은 직장에서 동료들과 소통하기 위해 소셜 네트워킹 사이트를 사용할 수 있어야 합니다."

IM3 I disagree that employees should be permitted to use social networking sites to communicate with their colleagues in the workplace. There are two reasons for this.

First, it would be so confusing and distracting. If we use social media at work, we will get lots of messages and it will seriously interrupt us when we need to concentrate.

Second, it will lower work productivity. That's because many employees would spend a great deal of time updating their profiles and sites. So, we need to use a separate messenger tool.

These are the reasons.

저는 직원들이 직장에서 동료들과 소통하기 위해 소셜 네트워킹 사이트를 사용하는 것을 허용해야 한다는 것에 동의하지 않습니다. 여기에는 두 가지 이유가 있습니다.

첫째, 그것은 매우 혼란스럽고 산만할 것입니다. 만약 우리가 직장에서 소셜 미디어를 사용한다면, 우리는 많은 메시지를 받을 것이고 우리가 집중해야 할 때 심각하게 방해가 될 것입니다.

둘째, 업무 생산성을 낮출 것입니다. 많은 직원이 프로필과 사이트를 업데이트하는 데 많은 시간을 할애하기 때문입니다. 그래서, 우리는 별도의 메신저 도구를 사용해야 합니다.

이것들이 그 이유입니다.

I disagree that employees should be permitted to use social networking sites to communicate with their colleagues in the workplace. There are two reasons for this.

First, it would be so confusing and distracting. If we use social media at work, we will get lots of messages even from people outside the company. Receiving too many notifications will seriously interrupt us when we need to concentrate.

Second, it will lower work productivity. That's because many employees would spend a great deal of time updating their profiles and sites throughout all-day. So, we need to introduce a separate messenger tool.

These are the reasons.

저는 직원들이 직장에서 동료들과 소통하기 위해 소셜 네트워킹 사이트를 사용하는 것을 허용해야 한다는 것에 동의하지 않습니다. 여기에는 두 가지 이유가 있습니다.

첫째, 그것은 매우 혼란스럽고 산만할 것입니다. 만약 우리가 직장에서 소셜 미디어를 사용한다면, 우리는 심지어 회사 밖의 사람들로부터도 많은 메시지를 받을 것입니다. 너무 많은 알림을 받는 것은 우리가 집중해야 할 때 우리를 심각하게 방해할 것입니다.

둘째, 업무 생산성을 낮출 것입니다. 많은 직원들이 하루 종일 프로필과 사이트를 업데이트하는 데 많은 시간을 할애하기 때문입니다. 그래서 우리는 별도의 메신저 도구를 도입해야 합니다.

이것들이 그 이유입니다.

I disagree that employees should be permitted to use social networking sites to communicate with their colleagues in the workplace. There are two reasons for this.

First, it would be so confusing and distracting. If we use social media at work, we will get lots of messages not only from colleagues but also from friends and family members. Receiving too many notifications will seriously interrupt us when we need to concentrate. So, using social networking sites should not be allowed at work.

Second, it will lower work productivity. That's because many employees would spend a great deal of time updating their profiles and sites throughout all-day. So, we need to introduce a separate messenger tool specially designed for office work.

These are the reasons.

저는 직원들이 직장에서 동료들과 소통하기 위해 소셜 네트워킹 사이트를 사용하는 것을 허용해야 한다는 것에 동의하지 않습니다. 여기에는 두 가지 이유가 있습니다.

첫째, 그것은 매우 혼란스럽고 산만할 것입니다. 만약 우리가 직장에서 소셜 미디어를 사용한다면, 우리는 동료들뿐만 아니라 친구들과 가족들로부터도 많은 메시지를 받을 것입니다. 너무 많은 알림을 받는 것은 우리가 집중해야 할 때 우리를 심각하게 방해할 것입니다. 따라서, 소셜 네트워킹 사이트를 사용하는 것이 직장에서 허용되어서는 안 됩니다.

둘째, 업무 생산성을 낮출 것입니다. 많은 직원들이 하루 종일 프로필과 사이트를 업데이트하는 데 많은 시간을 할애하기 때문입니다. 그래서 사무용으로 특별히 설계된 별도의 메신저 툴을 도입해야 합니다.

이것들이 그 이유입니다.

06 실전유형 모의고사

모범답변·템플릿

Question 1

Thank you for watching →/ Waterville local news. ↘// First, →/ we have your weather news. ↘// We will experience chilly and rainy days →/ today and tomorrow. ↘// However, →/ when we approach the weekend, →/ we will see →/ several extremely sunny days. ↘// Make sure to wear sunscreen, ↗/ a hat, ↗/ and sunglasses →/ to protect your skin and eyes. ↘//

Waterville 지역 뉴스를 시청해 주셔서 감사합니다. 먼저, 날씨 소식이 있겠습니다. 오늘과 내일은 쌀쌀하고 비가 오겠습니다. 하지만 주말에는 날씨가 매우 맑을 것입니다. 피부와 눈을 보호하기 위해 자외선 차단제, 모자, 선글라스를 꼭 착용하세요.

Question 2

Welcome to →/ the Sweet Surprise Chocolate factory. ↘// I hope →/ everybody is excited →/ to get an inside look →/ at the process of manufacturing. ↘// During the tour, →/ you will see →/ how chocolates are mixed, ↗/ molded, ↗/ and packaged. ↘// When we have finished →/ touring the factory, →/ everyone will receive →/ a complimentary assortment →/ of candy. ↘//

Sweet Surprise 초콜릿 공장에 오신 것을 환영합니다. 모든 분들께서는 제조과정 견학을 기대하시길 바랍니다. 투어 기간 동안, 여러분은 초콜릿이 어떻게 섞이고, 찍어지고, 포장되는지를 보게 될 것입니다. 공장 견학을 마치면, 모든 분들은 무료로 사탕 세트를 받아 가실 수 있습니다.

| 장소 | This picture was taken in a kitchen. | 이 사진은 주방에서 찍혔습니다. |

| 인원 | There are two people. | 이 장면에는 두 사람이 있습니다. |

| 중심 대상 | A man is washing the dishes. Next to him, a woman is wiping the dish with a dishcloth. | 남자는 설거지를 하고 있습니다. 그 남자 옆에는 한 여성이 행주로 접시를 닦고 있습니다. |

| 주변 대상 | In the background, I can see cups, dishes, and white drawers. | 배경에는 컵, 접시, 서랍장들이 보입니다. |

| 상황 | Overall, it seems like those people are concentrating on dishwashing. | 전반적으로 그들은 설거지에 집중하고 있는 것 같습니다. |

Question 4

장소	This picture was taken at a cafe.	이 사진은 카페에서 찍힌 사진입니다.
인원	There are two women in the picture.	사진 속에는 두 명의 여자가 있습니다.
중심 대상	On the left, the woman is studying something on her computer and taking notes.	왼쪽에는 여자가 컴퓨터로 무언가를 공부하며 메모를 하고 있습니다.
주변 대상	Next to her, the other woman is standing while looking at the monitor and holding a book.	그녀 옆에 또 다른 여자가 모니터를 보며 책을 들고 서 있습니다.
상황	Overall, it seems like they are having a tutoring session.	전반적으로 그들은 과외를 하고 있는 것 같습니다.

🔊 Imagine a magazine publisher is conducting research in your area about organizing family events such as weddings or birthday parties. You have agreed to participate in a telephone interview about organizing family events.

한 잡지 출판사가 결혼식이나 생일 파티와 같은 가족 행사를 주관하는 것에 대해 당신의 지역에서 연구를 하고 있다고 가정해 보십시오. 당신은 가족 행사 준비에 관한 전화 인터뷰에 참여하기로 동의했습니다.

Question 5

Q What was the family event you last attended, and where was it held?

마지막으로 참석했던 가족 행사는 무엇이고, 어디서 열렸나요?

A The family event I last attended was my cousin's birthday party, and we had the party at a nice restaurant.

마지막으로 참석한 가족 행사는 사촌 생일 파티였고, 우리는 근사한 레스토랑에서 파티를 했습니다.

Question 6

Q How much time did you spend attending the last family event, and what kind of food was served?

지난 가족 행사에서 얼마나 많은 시간을 보냈고, 어떤 음식이 제공되었나요?

A I spent about 2 hours at the birthday party, and we had steaks and hamburgers.

저는 생일파티에서 2시간 정도 보냈고, 저희는 스테이크와 햄버거를 먹었습니다.

Q If you were in charge of organizing a family event, what kind of event would you like to hold, and why?

가족 행사를 주관한다면 어떤 행사를 개최하고 싶으며, 그 이유는 무엇입니까?

IM3-IH If I were in charge of organizing a family event, I would hold a family movie night, and here is why.

First, it's a fun way to gather everyone for a relaxing evening.

Also, it's easy to prepare. I can simply set up a projector and choose a movie.

That's all.

제가 가족 행사를 주관한다면 가족 영화의 밤을 열 것이고, 여기 그 이유가 있습니다.

첫째, 편안한 저녁을 위해 모두가 모일 수 있는 즐거운 방법입니다.

또한 그것은 준비하기 쉽습니다. 저는 간단히 프로젝터를 설치하고 영화를 고르면 됩니다.

이상입니다.

AL-AH If I were in charge of organizing a family event, I would hold a family movie night, and here is why.

First, it's a fun way to gather every family member together for a relaxing evening.

Also, it's easy to prepare. All I need to do is set up a projector in my living room, buy their favorite snacks, and choose a family-friendly movie that everyone can enjoy. I bet my family will love it.

제가 가족 행사를 주관한다면 가족 영화의 밤을 열 것이고, 여기 그 이유가 있습니다.

첫째, 그것은 편안한 저녁을 위해 모든 가족 구성원들을 함께 모으는 즐거운 방법입니다.

또한 그것은 준비하기 쉽습니다. 제가 해야 할 일은 거실에 프로젝터를 설치하고, 그들이 가장 좋아하는 간식을 사고, 모두가 즐길 수 있는 가족 친화적인 영화를 선택하는 것 뿐입니다. 분명 우리 가족들이 좋아할 것입니다.

Wilson Community Center

Spring term: April 3 - May 21, Deadline for registration: March 12

Photography class - basic level	Mondays	2:30 - 3:30 P.M.
Italian cooking: desserts	Tuesdays	1:30 - 2:30 P.M.
Pottery class - advanced level	Wednesdays	4:30 - 5:30 P.M.
Japanese cooking: soups	Thursdays	1:00 - 2:00 P.M.
Water painting	Fridays	2:00 - 3:30 P.M.
Guitar - intermediate level	Saturdays	10:00 - 11:30 A.M.

Costs: 150$/course (Saturday courses - 100$)

🔊 Hi, I am very interested in the Wilson Community Center courses in the spring term. Can I ask a few questions about its schedule?

안녕하세요. 저는 Wilson Community Center에서 하는 봄 학기 수업들에 관심이 많습니다. 이 일정에 대해 몇 가지 물어봐도 될까요?

Question 8

Q When does the spring term begin and when does it end?

봄 학기는 언제 시작되고, 언제 끝납니까?

A The spring term begins on April 3rd and it ends on May 21st.

봄 학기는 4월 3일에 시작되고 5월 21일에 끝납니다.

Question 9

Q I heard that it costs 100 dollars per course. Is that right?

한 수업당 100달러라고 들었습니다. 이것이 맞습니까?

A No, actually, it costs 150 dollars per course. But if you take a course on Saturdays, it's 100 dollars.

아니요, 사실 한 수업당 150달러입니다. 하지만 토요일에 수업을 들으신다면 100달러입니다.

Question 10

Q I am very interested in cooking classes. Could you give me all the details of the cooking classes that you will be offering?

저는 요리 수업에 관심이 많습니다. 제공되는 요리 수업들에 대한 모든 세부사항을 저에게 알려주시겠어요?

A Sure, there are two cooking classes. First, there is an Italian cooking class on Tuesdays from 1:30 to 2:30 P.M. and we will learn how to make Italian desserts. Second, there is a Japanese cooking class on Thursdays from 1:00 to 2:00 P.M. and we will learn how to make Japanese soups.

물론이죠. 두 개의 요리 수업이 있습니다. 먼저, 화요일 오후 1시 반부터 2시 반까지 Italian cooking class가 있고 이탈리안 디저트 만드는 법을 배울 것입니다. 둘째로는 목요일 오후 1시부터 2시까지 Japanese cooking class가 있고 일식 국 만드는 법을 배울 것입니다.

Question 11

🔊 For high school students, what are the advantages of acting in theater performances?

고등학생들이 연극 공연을 하는 것의 장점은 무엇입니까?

IM3 There are some advantages of acting in theater performances for high school students.

First, it's a good chance to relieve stress and relax because it's an exciting experience that they can't get in the classroom.

Second, while acting, they may express their inner emotions that they feel uncomfortable sharing about, such as depression or anxiety.

These are the advantages of acting in theater performances for high school students.

고등학생들이 연극 공연을 하는 것에는 몇 가지 장점이 있습니다.

첫째, 교실에서는 얻을 수 없는 신나는 경험이기 때문에 스트레스를 풀고 휴식을 취할 수 있는 좋은 기회입니다.

둘째, 그들은 연기를 하면서 우울증이나 불안감과 같이 그들이 공유하는 것에 대해 불편함을 느끼는 내면의 감정을 표현할 수 있습니다.

이것들이 고등학생들이 연극 공연을 하는 것의 장점입니다.

There are some advantages of acting in theater performances for high school students.

First, it's a good chance to relieve stress and relax because it's an exciting experience that they can't get in the classroom. I think it will be helpful for them to have some time to escape from their daily routines.

Second, while acting, they may express their inner emotions that they feel uncomfortable sharing about, such as depression or anxiety. This activity will improve their mental health.

These are the advantages of acting in theater performances for high school students.

고등학생들이 연극 공연을 하는 것에는 몇 가지 장점이 있습니다.

첫째, 교실에서는 얻을 수 없는 신나는 경험이기 때문에 스트레스를 풀고 휴식을 취할 수 있는 좋은 기회입니다. 저는 그들이 일상에서 벗어날 수 있는 시간을 갖는 것이 도움이 될 것이라고 생각합니다.

둘째, 그들은 연기를 하면서 우울증이나 불안감과 같이 그들이 공유하는 것에 대해 불편함을 느끼는 내면의 감정을 표현할 수 있습니다. 이 활동은 그들의 정신 건강을 향상시킬 것입니다.

이것들이 고등학생들이 연극 공연을 하는 것의 장점입니다.

AL-AH There are some advantages of acting in theater performances for high school students.

First, it's a good chance to relieve stress and relax because it's an exciting experience that they can't get in the classroom. These days, high school students are under heavy academic pressure and suffering from extreme stress. So, it will be helpful for them to have some time to escape from their daily routines.

Second, while acting, they may express their inner emotions that they feel uncomfortable sharing about, such as depression or anxiety. This activity will improve their mental health and help students to study in a better mood.

These are the advantages of acting in theater performances for high school students.

고등학생들이 연극 공연을 하는 것에는 몇 가지 장점이 있습니다.

첫째, 교실에서는 얻을 수 없는 신나는 경험이기 때문에 스트레스를 풀고 휴식을 취할 수 있는 좋은 기회입니다. 요즘, 고등학생들은 극심한 학업 압박을 받고 극심한 스트레스를 받고 있습니다. 따라서, 그들이 일상생활에서 벗어날 수 있는 시간을 갖는 것은 도움이 될 것입니다.

둘째, 그들은 연기를 하면서 우울증이나 불안감과 같이 그들이 공유하는 것에 대해 불편함을 느끼는 내면의 감정을 표현할 수 있습니다. 이 활동은 그들의 정신 건강을 향상시키고 학생들이 더 나은 기분으로 공부하도록 도울 것입니다.

이것들이 고등학생들이 연극 공연을 하는 것의 장점입니다.

07

실전유형 모의고사

모범답변·템플릿

Question 1

This Sunday, →/ visit Jackson Grocery →/ for our tenth-anniversary celebration. ↘// Enjoy free dessert, ↗/ games, ↗/ and music →/ in the store parking lot. ↘// Also, →/ come watch →/ famous chef and cookbook author →/ Pete Evans →/ cook delicious foods. ↘// The party starts at 10 A.M. →/ at Jackson Grocery, →/ located at Bank Road, →/ Law Avenue. ↘//

이번 주 일요일, Jackson Grocery의 10주년 행사에 방문해보세요. 매장 주차장에서 무료 디저트, 게임, 그리고 음악을 즐기세요. 또한, 유명 요리사이자 요리책 작가인 Pete Evans가 맛있는 음식을 요리하는 것을 보러 오세요. 이 파티는 오전 10시에 Bank road, Law avenue에 위치한 Jackson Grocery에서 시작합니다.

Question 2

Hello, →/ and thank you for contacting →/ Samantha's cooking class. ↘// We will go through →/ some major renovations →/ for a few weeks. ↘// All of our ovens, ↗/ fridges, ↗/ and utensils →/ will be replaced. ↘// As a result, →/ classes will be closed →/ until the works are finished. ↘// To see updates →/ on our progress, →/ please visit our website. ↘//

안녕하세요, Samantha의 요리교실에 연락 주셔서 감사합니다. 우리는 몇 주 동안 대대적인 보수 공사를 할 예정입니다. 저희의 모든 오븐, 냉장고, 그리고 식기도구들이 교체될 것입니다. 그러므로 공사가 끝날 때까지 수업들이 중단될 것입니다. 진행 현황에 대한 이메일 업데이트를 보시려면 저희 웹사이트를 방문해 주십시오.

Question 3

장소	This picture was taken at a clothing store.	이 사진은 옷가게에서 찍혔습니다.

인원	There are two women.	두 여성이 있습니다.

중심 대상	A woman in the center is listening to music using earphones. In the foreground, the other woman is looking at something.	중앙에 있는 여자는 이어폰으로 음악을 듣고 있습니다. 전방에는 다른 여자가 무언가를 보고 있습니다.

주변 대상	In the background, various clothes are displayed.	배경에는 다양한 옷이 진열되어 있습니다.

상황	Overall, it seems like those women are shopping for clothes.	전반적으로 두 여성은 옷 쇼핑을 하고 있는 것 같습니다.

Question 4

장소	This picture was <u>taken at a hotel</u>.	이 사진은 호텔에서 찍었습니다.

인원	There are three people.	이 사진 속에는 세 사람이 있습니다.

중심 대상	On the left, a young couple is <u>standing at the reception</u>. And a man is <u>giving a card</u> to an employee. On the right, the employee is <u>receiving a card</u>.	왼쪽에는 젊은 커플이 리셉션에 서있습니다. 그리고 남성은 직원에게 카드를 주고 있습니다. 우측에는 직원이 카드를 받고 있습니다.

주변 대상	In the background, I can see a plant and curtains.	배경에는 식물과 커튼이 보입니다.

상황	Overall, it seems like the couple is <u>checking in at the hotel</u>.	전반적으로 이 커플은 호텔에서 체크인을 하고 있는 것 같습니다.

🔊 Imagine an interior magazine publisher is conducting research in your area about renting a house. You have agreed to participate in a telephone interview about renting a house.

한 인테리어 잡지사가 당신의 동네에서 집을 임차하는 것에 대한 연구를 하고 있다고 가정해 보십시오. 당신은 집 임차에 관한 전화 인터뷰에 참여하기로 동의했습니다.

Question 5

Q Is it easy to find a house to rent in your area? Why or why not?

당신의 동네에서 임차할 집을 찾는 것이 쉽습니까? 그 이유는 무엇입니까?

A No, it isn't because there are not many houses in my town.

아니요, 저희 동네에는 집들이 많이 없기 때문에 쉽지 않습니다.

Question 6

Q If you were looking for a house to rent, would you want your friend to visit the house with you, or would you like to go alone, and why?

만약 당신이 임차할 집을 찾는다면 그 집에 친구와 함께 가길 원하나요? 아니면 혼자 가는 것을 원하나요? 그 이유는 무엇인가요?

A In that case, I would go there with my friends because I need someone to share opinions about it.

그 상황에는, 제 친구들과 갈 것입니다. 왜냐하면 집에 대한 의견을 나눌 누군가가 필요하기 때문입니다.

Question 7

Q When choosing a house to live in, which of the following is the most important consideration for you and why?

- Whether a shopping center is located nearby or not
- Whether public transportation is close or not
- Whether having pets is allowed or not

거주할 집을 선택할 때 다음 중 당신에게 가장 중요한 고려사항은 무엇이며, 그 이유는 무엇입니까?

- 쇼핑센터가 근처에 있는지 여부
- 대중교통이 가까운지 여부
- 애완동물 허용 여부

IM3-IH For me, whether public transportation is close or not is the most important consideration, and here is why.

First, if I live close to public transportation, <u>commuting is convenient</u>.

Second, it's cost-effective because <u>I can save the expense of driving</u>.

This is why.

저에게는 대중교통이 가까운지 여부가 가장 중요한 고려 사항이고, 이유는 이러합니다.

첫째, 대중교통과 가까운 곳에 살면 출퇴근이 편리합니다.

둘째, 운전 비용을 절약할 수 있기 때문에 비용 효율적입니다.

이것이 그 이유입니다.

AL-AH For me, whether public transportation is close or not is the most important consideration, and here is why.

First, if I live close to public transportation, <u>commuting is convenient</u>. Then, I can save time and energy when going to work.

Second, it's cost-effective. Since public transportation offers convenient access to a variety of destinations such as work, school, shopping, and entertainment, <u>I can save the expense of driving</u>.

This is why.

저에게는 대중교통이 가까운지 여부가 가장 중요한 고려 사항이고, 이유는 이러합니다.

첫째, 대중교통과 가까운 곳에 살면 통근이 편리합니다. 그러면 저는 출근할 때 시간과 에너지를 절약할 수 있습니다.

둘째, 비용 효율적입니다. 대중교통으로 직장, 학교, 쇼핑, 오락 등 다양한 목적지에 편리하게 갈 수 있기 때문에 저는 운전 비용을 절약할 수 있습니다.

이것이 그 이유입니다.

Business association – Quarterly seminar		
Daven hotel, Seminar fee: 90$ in advance, 110$ at the seminar		
9:30 A.M. – 10:30 A.M.	Registration	–
10:30 A.M. – 11:30 A.M.	Keynote speech: your target audience	Hailey Pitt
11:30 A.M. – 12:30 P.M.	Lecture: importance of customer loyalty	Donald Cho
12:30 P.M. – 1:30 P.M.	Lunch (Buffet - Holly restaurant)	–
1:30 P.M. – 2:30 P.M.	Discussion: marketing trends	Alice Molina
2:30 P.M. – 3:30 P.M.	Workshop: building brand awareness	Donald Cho

🔊 Hi, I am very interested in the quarterly seminar of the business association. Can I ask a few questions about its schedule?

안녕하세요. 저는 Business association의 Quarterly seminar에 관심이 많습니다. 이 일정에 대해 몇 가지 물어봐도 될까요?

Question 8

Q What time will the keynote speech start, and what is the title of it?

Keynote speech는 몇 시에 시작하며, 제목은 무엇인가요?

A The keynote speech will start at 10:30 A.M., and its title is your target audience.

Keynote speech는 오전 10시 반에 시작할 것이고, 제목은 your target audience입니다.

Question 9

Q As far as I know, the registration fee is the same, even if I register on the day of the seminar. Is that right?

세미나 당일에 등록을 해도 등록비는 동일하다고 알고 있습니다. 맞습니까?

A No, actually, if you register in advance, it's 90 dollars. But if you register at the seminar, it's 110 dollars.

아닙니다. 사실 미리 등록을 하시면 90달러입니다. 하지만 세미나 당일에 등록하시면 110달러입니다.

Question 10

Q I am very interested in Donald Cho's talk. Could you give me all the details of the sessions led by Donald Cho?

저는 Donald Cho의 강연에 관심이 많습니다. Donald Cho가 진행할 세션의 모든 세부사항을 알려 주시겠어요?

A Sure, there are two sessions. First, from 11:30 A.M. to 12:30 P.M., there is a lecture on the importance of customer loyalty by Donald Cho. Second, from 2:30 P.M. to 3:30 P.M., there is a workshop about building brand awareness by Donald Cho.

물론이죠. 두 개의 세션이 있습니다. 먼저, 오전 11시 반부터 오후 12시 반까지 Donald Cho의 importance of customer loyalty 강의가 있습니다. 두 번째로, 오후 2시 반부터 3시 반까지 Donald Cho가 진행하는 building brand awareness에 관한 워크숍이 있습니다.

🔊 What are the benefits of planning for a trip in advance?

여행계획을 미리 세우는 것의 장점은 무엇인가요?

IM3　There are some advantages of planning for a trip in advance.

First, planning ahead will allow us to find the best prices and possible discounts for airfare and rentals.

Second, it gives us pleasure because planning for a vacation itself is enjoyable. Just imagining the traveling sites and exotic foods itself excites us.

These are the advantages.

여행을 미리 계획하는 것에는 몇 가지 이점이 있습니다.

첫째, 미리 계획을 세우면 항공료와 임대료에 대한 최적의 가격과 가능한 할인을 찾을 수 있습니다.

둘째, 휴가 계획 자체가 재미있기 때문에 우리에게 즐거움을 줍니다. 여행지와 이국적인 음식들을 상상하는 것만으로도 우리는 신나게 됩니다.

이것들이 장점입니다.

IH

There are some advantages of planning for a trip in advance.

First, planning ahead will allow us to find the best prices and possible discounts for airfare and rentals. It's because traveling fares vary greatly depending on the season of the year.

Second, it gives us pleasure because planning for a vacation itself is enjoyable. Just imagining the traveling sites and exotic foods will make us excited before the trip.

These are the advantages.

여행을 미리 계획하는 것에는 몇 가지 이점이 있습니다.

첫째, 미리 계획을 세우면 항공료와 임대료에 대한 최적의 가격과 가능한 할인을 찾을 수 있습니다. 계절에 따라 여행 요금이 많이 다르기 때문입니다.

둘째, 휴가 계획 자체가 재미있기 때문에 우리에게 즐거움을 줍니다. 여행지와 이국적인 음식들을 상상하는 것만으로도 우리는 여행 전부터 신날 것입니다.

이것들이 장점입니다.

AL-AH

There are some advantages of planning for a trip in advance.

First, planning ahead will allow us to find the best prices and possible discounts for airfare and rentals. Since traveling fares vary greatly depending on the season of the year, planning ahead is crucial if seeking for economic benefits.

Second, it gives us pleasure because planning for a vacation itself is enjoyable. Just imagining the traveling sites and exotic foods will make us excited before the trip. So, we can enjoy the vibe of traveling earlier.

These are the advantages.

여행을 미리 계획하는 것에는 몇 가지 이점이 있습니다.

첫째, 미리 계획을 세우면 항공료와 임대료에 대한 최적의 가격과 가능한 할인을 찾을 수 있습니다. 계절에 따라 여행 요금이 크게 차이가 나기 때문에 경제적 이익을 추구한다면 미리 계획을 세우는 것이 중요합니다.

둘째, 휴가 계획 자체가 재미있기 때문에 우리에게 즐거움을 줍니다. 여행지와 이국적인 음식들을 상상하는 것만으로도 우리는 여행 전부터 신날 것입니다. 그래서 우리는 더 일찍 여행의 분위기를 즐길 수 있습니다.

이것들이 장점입니다.

08 실전유형 모의고사

모범답변·템플릿

Question 1

In local news, →/ the area restaurant Jay's pizza →/ will be closing next month. ↘// Jay Davis, →/ the owner of the restaurant, →/ opened the store →/ thirty years ago. ↘// Over the years, →/ it became →/ one of Chicago's most popular places →/ for catering, ↗/ birthday parties, ↗/ and other celebrations. ↘//

현지 뉴스에 따르면, 이 지역 레스토랑인 Jay's pizza는 다음 달 문을 닫습니다. 이 식당의 주인인 Jay Davis는 30년 전에 이 가게를 열었습니다. 그 시간 동안, 이곳은 케이터링, 생일 파티, 그리고 다른 기념행사로 시카고의 가장 인기 있는 장소들 중 하나가 되었습니다.

Question 2

Attention commuters. ↘// The trains →/ on the red line →/ are fifty minutes behind schedule. ↘// If you are traveling →/ on the red line, →/ consider taking an alternative →/ to your destination. ↘// Remember, →/ transit passes offer →/ full access to all the trains, ↗/ buses, ↗/ and street cars. ↘//

통근자분들 주목해 주세요. 레드 라인의 열차는 예정보다 50분 늦게 도착합니다. 레드 라인을 이용하시는 분은 목적지까지 가는 다른 방안을 고려해 보세요. 환승권으로 모든 기차, 버스 그리고 시내 전차를 이용할 수 있는 것을 기억해 주세요.

장소	This picture was <u>taken at a cafe</u>.	이 사진은 카페에서 찍은 사진입니다.
인원	There are two people.	두 사람이 있습니다.
중심 대상	In the front, a woman is <u>cleaning the coffee machine</u> using a brush. In the back, a man is <u>wiping another coffee machine</u> with a cloth.	앞쪽에서는 한 여자가 브러시를 이용해 커피 머신을 닦고 있습니다. 뒤쪽에서는 한 남자가 헝겊으로 다른 커피 머신을 닦고 있습니다.
주변 대상	They are both <u>focusing on their work</u>.	그들은 일에 집중하고 있습니다.
상황	Overall, it seems like they are <u>getting ready for business</u>.	전반적으로 그들은 장사 준비를 하고 있는 것 같습니다.

Question 4

장소 + 인원	There are three people in the buffet restaurant.	뷔페식당 안에 세 사람이 있습니다.
중심 대상 + 주변 대상	In the foreground, some dishes and bowls are displayed on the buffet table. On the left, a woman is reaching for a bowl. In the center, a chef is putting food on a plate. On the right, a man is picking up some food with tongs.	전방에는 뷔페 테이블 위에 몇 가지 요리와 그릇이 전시되어 있습니다. 왼쪽에는 여자가 그릇에 손을 뻗고 있습니다. 중앙에서, 요리사가 음식을 접시에 담고 있습니다. 오른쪽에는 한 남자가 집게로 음식을 집고 있습니다.
상황	Overall, it's a common scene of a buffet restaurant.	전반적으로 뷔페 식당의 흔한 풍경입니다.

Imagine a marketing firm is conducting research about health and fitness, and you have agreed to participate in a telephone interview about it.

마케팅 회사에서 건강 및 피트니스에 대한 연구를 수행하고 있으며, 당신은 이에 대한 전화 인터뷰에 참여하기로 동의했다고 가정해 보십시오.

Question 5

Q How often do you exercise, and who do you usually exercise with?

얼마나 자주 운동하세요? 보통 누구와 운동을 하시나요?

A I work out twice a week and I usually exercise with my personal trainer.

저는 일주일에 두 번 운동을 하며 보통 개인 트레이너와 함께 운동을 합니다.

Question 6

Q What is your favorite type of exercise, and where do you usually do that exercise?

가장 좋아하는 운동은 무엇인가요? 보통 어디서 그 운동을 하세요?

A My favorite exercise is weight training and cardio and I usually do those at the gym.

제가 가장 좋아하는 운동은 근력 운동과 유산소 운동이고, 주로 헬스장에서 운동합니다.

Question 7

Q What are the advantages of group exercise over working out alone?

단체 운동은 혼자 운동하는 것에 비해 어떤 장점이 있나요?

IM3-IH There are some advantages of group exercise.

First, it's motivating. For instance, group exercise gives support from others.

Second, I can learn better. Group exercise courses offer proper skills from a qualified instructor.

These are the advantages.

단체 운동에는 몇 가지 이점이 있습니다.

첫째, 동기부여가 됩니다. 예를 들어 단체 운동을 하면 다른 사람들로부터 도움을 받을 수 있습니다.

둘째, 저는 더 잘 배울 수 있습니다. 단체 운동 수업에서는 실력 있는 강사가 적절한 스킬을 알려줍니다.

이것들이 장점입니다.

AL-AH There are some advantages of group exercise over working out alone.

First, it's motivating. For instance, group exercise gives support from the instructor and other participants. This encouragement makes me stay committed to my fitness goal.

Second, I can learn better. Group exercise courses offer proper skills and techniques from a qualified instructor. Also, I can ask questions and get personalized feedback.

These are the advantages.

단체 운동은 혼자 운동하는 것보다 몇 가지 장점이 있습니다.

첫째, 동기부여가 됩니다. 예를 들어 단체 운동을 하면 강사와 다른 사람들로부터 도움을 받을 수 있습니다. 이 격려는 제가 체력 목표에 전념하도록 만듭니다.

둘째, 저는 더 잘 배울 수 있습니다. 단체 운동 수업에서는 실력 있는 강사가 적절한 스킬과 테크닉을 알려줍니다. 또한 저는 질문을 할 수 있고 개인 맞춤화된 피드백을 받을 수 있습니다.

이것들이 장점입니다.

International Conference of Video Game Industry	
Friday, March 3, Carol Conference Center	
9:00 – 10:00 A.M.	Opening remarks (conference organizer)
10:00 – 11:00 A.M.	Educational video games for class (Room 220)
11:00 A.M. – 12:30 P.M.	Top.10 video games in Asia (Room 110)
12:30 – 1:30 P.M.	Events for games: upcoming events (Room 240)
1:30 – 2:30 P.M.	Lists of gaming conventions (Room 310)
2:30 – 3:30 P.M.	Recent trends on educational video games (Room 115)
3:30 – 5:00 P.M.	Outstanding video game developers (Room 410)

🔊 Hi, I hope you could give me some information about the international conference of the video game industry.

안녕하세요, 비디오 게임 산업의 국제회의에 대해 정보를 좀 주셨으면 합니다.

Question 8

Q On what day will the conference be held, and what time will the first session start?

회의 날짜는 며칠입니까? 첫 번째 세션은 몇 시에 시작합니까?

A The conference will be held on Friday March 3rd and the first session will start at 9:00 A.M.

회의는 3월 3일 금요일에 열리며, 첫 번째 세션은 오전 9시에 시작합니다.

Q I heard that the conference is two-day long. Is that correct?

컨퍼런스가 이틀 동안 진행된다고 들었습니다. 맞나요?

A I am afraid not. The conference is one-day long which means it will take place for a day. Please keep that in mind.

아닙니다. 회의는 하루 동안 열리는 단일 일정입니다. 이 점을 명심해 주세요.

Q Could you give me all the details of the sessions that deal with educational video games?

교육용 비디오 게임을 다루는 세션의 모든 세부사항을 알려주시겠어요?

A Sure, there are two. The first one is 'Educational video games for class', and it will take place from 10:00 to 11:00 A.M. in room two-twenty. The second one is 'Recent trends on educational video games', and it will be held from 2:30 to 3:30 P.M. in room one-fifteen. That's all.

물론입니다. 두 가지 세션이 있습니다. 첫 번째는 '수업을 위한 교육 비디오 게임'이고 220호에서 오전 10시부터 11시까지 진행됩니다. 두 번째는 '교육 비디오 게임의 최근 트렌드'이며 115호에서 오후 2시 30분부터 3시 30분까지 진행될 예정입니다. 이상입니다.

Question 11

🔊 Do you agree that leaders should have strong time-management skills?

리더들은 뛰어난 시간 관리 능력을 갖춰야 한다는 것에 동의합니까?

IM3 I agree that leaders should have strong time-management skills. There are two reasons.

First, a leader with strong time management skills can figure out what is more important and urgent in a given situation. In other words, the leader knows work priorities.

Second, the leader can multitask better. For example, the leader can plan ahead for work and give team members a more detailed and timelier to-do list.

These are the reasons.

저는 리더가 뛰어난 시간 관리 능력을 갖춰야 한다는 것에 동의합니다. 두 가지 이유가 있습니다.

첫째, 뛰어난 시간 관리 능력을 가진 리더는 주어진 상황에서 무엇이 더 중요하고 시급한지 파악할 수 있습니다. 즉, 그 리더는 업무의 우선순위를 압니다.

둘째, 리더는 멀티태스킹을 더 잘 할 수 있습니다. 예를 들어, 리더는 일을 미리 계획하고 팀원들에게 보다 상세하고 시기적절한 업무 일정을 제공할 수 있습니다.

이것들이 그 이유입니다.

I agree that leaders should have strong time-management skills. There are two reasons.

First, a leader with strong time management skills can figure out what is more important and urgent in a given situation. In other words, the leader knows work priorities. This ability will reduce mistakes and the trial-and-error processes.

Second, the leader can multitask better. For example, the leader can plan ahead for work and give team members a more detailed and timelier to-do list. As a result, it will help the team meet the deadlines successfully and complete the work on time.

These are the reasons.

저는 리더가 뛰어난 시간 관리 능력을 갖춰야 한다는 것에 동의합니다. 두 가지 이유가 있습니다.

첫째, 뛰어난 시간 관리 능력을 가진 리더는 주어진 상황에서 무엇이 더 중요하고 시급한지 파악할 수 있습니다. 즉, 그 리더는 업무의 우선순위를 압니다. 이 능력을 통해 실수와 시행착오 프로세스를 줄일 수 있습니다.

둘째, 리더는 멀티태스킹을 더 잘 할 수 있습니다. 예를 들어, 리더는 일을 미리 계획하고 팀원들에게 보다 상세하고 시기적절한 업무 일정을 제공할 수 있습니다. 결과적으로, 팀이 마감일을 성공적으로 맞추고 제시간에 작업을 완료하는 데 도움이 될 것입니다.

이것들이 그 이유입니다.

AL-AH I agree that leaders should have strong time-management skills. There are two reasons.

First, a leader with strong time management skills can figure out what is more important and urgent in a given situation. In other words, the leader knows work priorities. This ability will reduce mistakes and the trial-and-error processes. Therefore, the team can work under an organized work plan.

Second, the leader can multitask better. For example, the leader can plan ahead for work and give team members a more detailed and timelier to-do list. As a result, it will help the team meet the deadlines successfully and complete the work on time.

These are the reasons.

저는 리더가 뛰어난 시간 관리 능력을 갖춰야 한다는 것에 동의합니다. 두 가지 이유가 있습니다.

첫째, 뛰어난 시간 관리 능력을 가진 리더는 주어진 상황에서 무엇이 더 중요하고 시급한지 파악할 수 있습니다. 즉, 그 리더는 업무의 우선순위를 압니다. 이 능력을 통해 실수와 시행착오 프로세스를 줄일 수 있습니다. 따라서, 팀은 체계적인 작업 계획에 따라 작업할 수 있습니다.

둘째, 리더는 멀티태스킹을 더 잘 할 수 있습니다. 예를 들어, 리더는 일을 미리 계획하고 팀원들에게 보다 상세하고 시기적절한 업무 일정을 제공할 수 있습니다. 결과적으로, 팀이 마감일을 성공적으로 맞추고 제시간에 작업을 완료하는 데 도움이 될 것입니다.

이것들이 그 이유입니다.

09 실전유형 모의고사

모범답변·템플릿

Question 1

In today's episode →/ of My Little Kitchen, →/ I will demonstrate →/ how to make →/ delicious tomato soup. ↘// To begin, →/ you will need →/ several fresh tomatoes. ↘// First, →/ simmer tomatoes, ↗/ butter, ↗/ and onion →/ until slightly thickened. ↘// Next, add a little water and blend everything together →/ just before serving. ↘// I recommend you serve this →/ with a slice of rosemary bread. ↘//

오늘 My Little Kitchen 에피소드에서는 맛있는 토마토 수프를 만드는 방법을 보여드리겠습니다. 우선, 신선한 토마토가 몇 개 필요합니다. 먼저 토마토, 버터, 양파를 약간 걸쭉해질 때까지 끓여줍니다. 다음으로, 서빙하기 바로 전에 물을 조금 넣고 모든 것을 함께 섞어주세요. 저는 이것을 로즈마리 빵 한 조각과 함께 내시는 것을 추천합니다.

Question 2

Good morning, →/ employees. ↘// We would like to introduce you to Mr. James Harden, →/ the new chairman →/ of this semiconductor company. ↘// In the past, →/ he's held senior positions →/ in many industries →/ including electronics, ↗/ technology, ↗/ and automotive. ↘// As you may know, →/ he's also been a member →/ of the National Semiconductor Council →/ for three years. ↘//

좋은 아침입니다, 직원 여러분. 이 반도체 회사의 새로운 회장, James harden씨를 소개합니다. 그는 과거에 전자, 기술, 자동차를 포함한 많은 산업에서 고위직을 역임했습니다. 아시다시피, 그는 또한 3년 동안 국가 반도체 협의회 위원을 역임했습니다.

Question 3

장소	This picture was taken at a clothing store.	이 사진은 옷 가게에서 찍힌 사진입니다.

인원	There are two women shopping for clothes.	옷을 사고 있는 두 명의 여자가 있습니다.

중심 대상	They are holding a sweater while smiling. It seems like the woman on the left is deciding whether to buy it or not.	그들은 웃으면서 스웨터를 들고 있습니다. 왼쪽의 여성이 이 옷을 살지 말지 결정하는 것 같아 보입니다.

주변 대상	In the background, various types of clothes are displayed on the racks.	배경에는 다양한 옷들이 선반에 진열되어 있습니다.

Question 4

장소	There are two men <u>in the office</u>.	사무실에 두 명의 남자가 있습니다.

중심 대상	They are sitting at the table <u>while</u> <u>chatting</u>. The man on the right is talking, and the other man is listening.	그들은 테이블에 앉아 대화 중입니다. 오 른쪽의 남성은 이야기를 하는 중이고, 또 다른 남성은 듣고 있는 중입니다.

주변 대상	On the table, I can see a laptop, glasses, and a small plant pot.	테이블 위에는 노트북, 물컵, 그리고 작은 화분이 보입니다.

상황	Overall, it seems like they are <u>working together</u> at the table.	전반적으로 그들은 테이블에서 함께 일 을 하고 있는 것 같습니다.

🔊 Imagine a lifestyle magazine is conducting research in your community about where you live. You have agreed to participate in a telephone interview about it.

라이프 스타일 잡지에서 당신이 사는 지역에 대한 연구를 수행하고 있다고 가정해 보십시오. 당신은 이와 관련된 전화 인터뷰에 참여하기로 동의했습니다.

Question 5

Q Where do you live, and how long have you lived there?

어디에 거주하고 있으며, 그곳에 거주하신지 얼마나 되었나요?

A I live in Seoul, Korea's capital city, and I've lived here for 3 years.

저는 대한민국의 수도인 서울에 살고 있고, 이곳에서 3년 동안 살았습니다.

Question 6

Q Where is the fun place to go in your area, and how often do you go there?

당신이 사는 지역에서 재미있는 장소는 어디입니까? 얼마나 자주 그곳을 가나요?

A When I want to entertain myself, I go to the City department store in my area, and I go there about once or twice a month.

즐겁게 놀고 싶을 때, 저는 동네 있는 시티 백화점에 가며, 한 달에 한두 번 정도 갑니다.

Q When deciding where to live, which of the following is the most important consideration, and why?

- Educational environment
- Access to the public transportation
- Size of the town

거주할 곳을 결정할 때 다음 중 가장 중요한 고려 사항은 무엇이며, 그 이유는 무엇입니까?

- 교육환경
- 대중교통 접근성
- 마을 규모

IM3-IH For me, the most important consideration is the size of the town, and here is why.

First, the cost of living depends on the size of the town.

Second, the town size could tell how many amenities are available.

This is why.

저에게 있어 가장 중요한 고려 사항은 마을의 규모이며, 여기 그 이유가 있습니다.

첫째, 생활비는 마을의 크기에 따라 달라집니다.

둘째, 마을의 규모는 얼마나 많은 편의시설을 이용할 수 있는지를 알려줍니다.

이것이 그 이유입니다.

AL-AH For me, the most important consideration is the size of the town, and here is why.

First, the cost of living depends on the size of the town. For instance, living expenses and prices in big cities are higher than those in small towns.

Second, the town size could tell how many amenities are available, such as shopping malls, restaurants, and cultural institutions.

This is why.

저에게 있어 가장 중요한 고려 사항은 마을의 규모이며, 여기 그 이유가 있습니다.

첫째, 생활비는 마을의 크기에 따라 달라집니다. 예를 들어 대도시의 생활비와 물가는 작은 도시의 생활비보다 높습니다.

둘째, 마을의 규모는 쇼핑몰, 식당, 문화 기관과 같은 편의시설을 얼마나 많이 이용할 수 있는지를 알려줍니다.

이것이 그 이유입니다.

Greenville Park

Events: June – August, Free unless noted

Event	Date	Time
Guided hike: Fame trail	June 15	2:00 – 3:00 P.M.
Family picnic	June 25	10:00 – 11:00 A.M.
Children camp night	July 9	4:00 – 5:00 P.M.
Talk: park history	July 30	1:00 – 2:00 P.M.
Dance competition	August 1	1:00 – 2:00 P.M.
Movie day	August 11	7:30 – 9:30 P.M.
Talk: identifying plants	August 29	3:30 – 4:30 P.M.

🔊 Hi, can I ask a few questions about the summer events at Greenville Park?

안녕하세요, 그린빌 파크에서 열리는 여름 행사에 대해 몇 가지 질문해도 될까요?

Question 8

Q What is the first event in June and what is the date of it?

6월의 첫 번째 행사는 무엇이며 날짜는 언제입니까?

A The first event in June is a guided hike at Fame trail, and the date of the event is June 15th.

6월 첫 번째 행사는 페임 트레일에서 진행되는 가이드와 함께 하는 하이킹이고, 날짜는 6월 15일입니다.

Question 9

Q I heard that the camp night will be in August, correct?

야간 캠프가 8월에 있다고 들었는데, 맞습니까?

A No, the children camp night will be on July 9th. Please keep that in mind.

아닙니다, 어린이 야간 캠프는 7월 9일에 있을 예정입니다. 이 점 명심해 주세요.

Question 10

Q Could you give me all the details of the talks during those summer events?

여름 행사 동안 있는 모든 강연에 대한 모든 세부 사항을 알려주시겠어요?

A Sure, there are two. The first one is about park history and it will be on July 30th from 1:00 to 2:00 P.M. The second one is about identifying plants and it will be on August 29th from 3:30 to 4:30 P.M. That's all.

물론이죠, 두 개 있습니다. 첫 번째는 공원 역사에 관한 것이고, 7월 30일 오후 1시부터 2시까지입니다. 두 번째 회담은 식물 식별하기에 관한 것이고, 8월 29일 오후 3시 30분부터 4시 30분까지입니다. 이상입니다.

🔊 Do you agree or disagree with the following statement?
"Salaries should be determined by skills only but not by how long a person has worked."

다음 명제에 동의하십니까, 동의하지 않으십니까?
"급여는 실력만으로 결정되어야 하며 얼마나 오래 일했는가에 의해서 결정되어서는 안 됩니다."

IM3 I disagree that salaries should be determined by skills only but not by how long a person has worked. There are two reasons for this.

First, it's risky. For example, <u>a person's skill can't tell everything about his or her qualifications</u>. Also, there's a lot to learn from experienced workers.

Second, skill is not everything. For example, <u>there are many essential aspects of an employee other than being skillful</u> such as sociability, work ethic, patience, and you name it.

These are the reasons.

급여는 실력만으로 결정되어야 하며 얼마나 오래 일했는가에 의해서 결정되어서는 안 된다는 것에 동의하지 않습니다. 두 가지 이유가 있습니다.

첫째, 위험합니다. 예를 들어, 누군가의 실력만으로 그 사람의 모든 자질을 판단할 수 없습니다. 또한 경험이 풍부한 경력자들로부터 배울 점이 많습니다.

둘째, 능력만이 다가 아닙니다. 예를 들어, 직원의 능력 외에도 사회성, 직업윤리, 인내심, 그 외 많은 필수적인 측면들이 있습니다.

이것들이 이유입니다.

IH

I disagree that salaries should be determined by skills only but not by how long a person has worked. There are two reasons for this.

First, it's risky. For example, a person's skill can't tell everything about his or her qualifications. I mean, how long a person has worked should be considered as well because there's a lot to learn from experienced workers.

Second, skill is not everything. For example, there are many essential aspects of an employee other than being skillful such as sociability, work ethic, patience, and you name it. These qualities often outweigh one's skills.

These are the reasons.

급여는 실력만으로 결정되어야 하며 얼마나 오래 일했는가에 의해서 결정되어서는 안 된다는 것에 동의하지 않습니다. 두 가지 이유가 있습니다.

첫째, 위험합니다. 예를 들어, 누군가의 실력만으로 그 사람의 모든 자질을 판단할 수 없습니다. 제 말은, 경력자에게서 배울 것이 많기 때문에 그 사람이 얼마나 오래 일했는지도 고려되어야 한다는 것입니다.

둘째, 능력만이 다가 아닙니다. 예를 들어, 직원의 능력 외에도 사회성, 직업윤리, 인내심, 그 외 많은 필수적인 측면들이 있습니다. 이러한 자질들은 종종 사람의 실력을 능가합니다.

이것들이 이유입니다.

AL-AH

I disagree that salaries should be determined by skills only but not by how long a person has worked. There are two reasons for this.

First, it's risky. For example, a person's skill can't tell everything about his or her qualifications. I mean, how long a person has worked should be considered as well because there's a lot to learn from experienced workers. You should never underestimate what you learn from your experience.

Second, because skill is not everything, one should be evaluated as a whole. For example, there are many essential aspects of an employee other than being skillful such as sociability, work ethic, patience, and you name it. These qualities often outweigh one's skills.

These are the reasons.

급여는 실력만으로 결정되어야 하며 얼마나 오래 일했는가에 의해서 결정되어서는 안 된다는 것에 동의하지 않습니다. 두 가지 이유가 있습니다.

첫째, 위험합니다. 예를 들어, 누군가의 실력만으로 그 사람의 모든 자질을 판단할 수 없습니다. 제 말은, 경력자에게서 배울 것이 많기 때문에 그 사람이 얼마나 오래 일했는지도 고려되어야 한다는 것입니다. 경험에서 배운 것을 결코 과소평가해서는 안 됩니다.

둘째, 능력만이 다가 아니기에 전체적으로 평가되어야 합니다. 예를 들어, 직원의 능력 외에도 사회성, 직업윤리, 인내심, 그 외 많은 필수적인 측면들이 있습니다. 이러한 자질들은 종종 사람의 실력을 능가합니다.

이것들이 이유입니다.

10

실전유형 모의고사

모범답변·템플릿

Question 1

Thank you for watching →/ Max and Milly's Morning TV show. ↘// Today, →/ we will speak →/ with a local musician →/ John Stanley, →/ who uses unusual instruments →/ to create exceptional sounds. ↘// But first, →/ let's check on breaking news, ↗/ weather, ↗/ and sports. ↘//

맥스와 밀리의 아침쇼를 시청해 주셔서 감사합니다. 오늘 우리는 특별한 소리를 내기 위해 특이한 악기를 사용하는 현지 음악가 John Stanley와 이야기를 나눌 것입니다. 하지만 먼저, 뉴스 속보, 날씨, 그리고 스포츠 소식을 살펴봅시다.

Question 2

Welcome to →/ the guided walking tour →/ to the Goldstone National Park. ↘// During the tour, →/ we will explore →/ the scenic trails, ↗/ experience the natural amenities, ↗/ and end with a light outdoor dinner. ↘// Before we begin, →/ I want to make sure →/ that everyone is wearing →/ appropriate clothing and footwear. ↘//

골드스톤 국립공원의 도보여행에 오신 것을 환영합니다. 관광하는 동안, 우리는 경치 좋은 산책로를 탐험하고, 자연 시설을 경험하고, 가벼운 야외 저녁식사로 마무리할 것입니다. 시작하기 전에, 저는 모든 분들이 적절한 옷과 신발을 착용하고 있는지 확인하고 싶습니다.

Question 3

장소	This picture was <u>taken on the street</u>.	이 사진은 거리에서 찍힌 사진입니다.
인원	Several cars are parked there, and an old couple is <u>walking on the street</u>.	이곳에는 몇 대의 차가 주차되어 있고, 한 노부부가 길을 걷고 있습니다.
중심 대상	The man on the left is <u>walking with a cane</u>, and the woman on the right is <u>talking on the phone</u>.	왼쪽에 있는 남자는 지팡이를 짚고 걷고 있고, 오른쪽에 있는 여자는 전화 통화를 하고 있습니다.
주변 대상	In the background, there are trees and buildings.	배경에는 나무와 건물들이 있습니다.

Question 4

장소	This picture was <u>taken at a library</u>.	이 사진은 도서관에서 찍힌 사진입니다.

인원	There are three people.	세 사람이 있습니다.

중심 대상	<u>In the foreground</u>, a woman is standing and picking up a book from the bookshelf. Behind her, two students are <u>studying together</u>.	전방에 한 여자가 서서 책꽂이에 있는 책을 집어 들고 있습니다. 그녀의 뒤에는 두 학생이 함께 공부하고 있습니다.

주변 대상	In the background, I can see many books on the shelves.	배경에는 책꽂이에 있는 많은 책들을 볼 수 있습니다.

상황	Overall, it's a <u>common scene in a library</u>.	전반적으로 이것은 도서관의 흔한 풍경입니다.

🔊 Imagine a marketing firm is conducting research in your area about life patterns. You have agreed to participate in a telephone interview about it.

라이프스타일 잡지가 당신의 지역에서 생활 패턴에 대한 조사를 하고 있다고 가정해 보세요. 당신은 이와 관련된 전화 인터뷰에 참여하기로 동의하셨습니다.

Question 5

Q What time does your work or school start? What time does it end?

당신의 일이나 학교는 몇 시에 시작합니까? 몇 시에 끝나요?

A I work from 9 to 6, but sometimes I work late when the workload is heavy.

저는 9시부터 6시까지 일합니다, 하지만 가끔 일이 많을 때는 늦게까지 일해요.

Question 6

Q Do you keep track of important schedules on your note or an electronic device, and why?

당신은 중요한 일정을 메모로 관리하나요? 아니면 전자 기기로 관리하나요? 그 이유는 무엇입니까?

A I keep track of important schedules on an electronic device because it's portable and safe for data management.

저는 중요한 일정을 전자 기기로 관리합니다. 왜냐하면 휴대성이 좋고 데이터를 관리하기에 안전하기 때문입니다.

Question 7

Q If an opportunity to change the time your workday or school day starts and ends is given, would you? Why or why not?

만약 당신의 근무일이나 학교가 시작하는 시간과 끝나는 시간을 바꿀 기회가 주어진다면 당신은 그렇게 하겠습니까? 그 이유는 무엇입니까?

IM3-IH No, I wouldn't take that opportunity, and here is why.

First, I work from 9 to 6, which perfectly works for me.

Second, if I reschedule my working time, the new schedule would confuse me.

This is why.

아니요, 저는 그 기회를 이용하지 않을 것이고, 여기 그 이유가 있습니다.

첫째, 저는 9시부터 6시까지 일을 하는데, 이것은 저에게 완벽하게 맞습니다.

둘째, 만약 제가 근무 시간을 재조정한다면 새로운 일정은 저를 혼란스럽게 할 것입니다.

이것이 그 이유입니다.

AL-AH No, I wouldn't take that opportunity, and here is why.

First, I work from 9 to 6, which perfectly works for me.
So, I don't need to make a change to it.

Second, if I reschedule my working time, I also need to change my work routines, and the new schedule would confuse me.
So, I wouldn't change when to start and end my work to avoid any confusion and disorder.

This is why.

아니요, 저는 그 기회를 이용하지 않을 것이고, 여기 그 이유가 있습니다.

첫째, 저는 9시부터 6시까지 일을 하는데, 이것은 저에게 완벽하게 맞습니다. 그래서 저는 그것을 바꿀 필요가 없습니다.

둘째, 만약 제가 일하는 시간을 재조정한다면 저는 저의 일과도 바꿔야 하고, 새로운 일정은 저를 혼란스럽게 할 것입니다. 그래서 저는 혼돈과 혼란을 피하기 위해 제 일을 언제 시작하고 언제 끝날지 바꾸지 않을 것입니다.

이것이 그 이유입니다.

Sales Employees Association Meeting
City Electronics / November 2 / Employee Lounge

9:00 – 10:00 A.M.	Breakfast	–
10:00 – 11:00 A.M.	Employee Orientation	Rose Kinder
11:00 A.M. – Noon	Store tour	James Aron
Noon – 1:00 P.M.	Lunch	–
1:00 – 2:00 P.M.	Video: customer satisfaction (Includes quizzes for trainees)	Brad Tailor
2:00 – 3:00 P.M.	Lecture: customer-driven mind	Akiko Nami
3:00 – 4:00 P.M.	Video: communication skills (Includes networking)	Nina Simon

🔊 Hi, I hope you could give me some information about the sales-employees association meeting at City electronics.

안녕하세요, 시티 일렉트로닉스에서 열리는 영업 사원 협회 회의에 대한 정보를 좀 주셨으면 합니다.

Question 8

Q What time does employee orientation start, and who will be leading it?

직원 오리엔테이션은 몇 시에 시작하며, 누가 진행하나요?

A The employee orientation starts at 10:00 A.M. and Rose Kinder will be leading it.

직원 오리엔테이션은 오전 10시에 시작하고 Rose Kinder가 진행할 겁니다.

Q I heard that there will be a store tour during the meeting, but no one will lead the session. Is that right?

회의 중에 매장 투어가 있을 거라고 들었는데, 아무도 진행을 안 하는 게 맞습니까?

A No, I'm afraid you have the wrong information. James Aron will lead the store tour from 11:00 A.M. to noon.

아니요, 잘못 알고 계신 것 같습니다. James Aron이 오전 11시부터 정오까지 매장 투어를 진행할 예정입니다.

Q Could you give me all the details of the sessions that we will watch a video?

비디오를 보는 세션에 대한 모든 세부 사항을 알려주시겠습니까?

A Sure. First, from 1:00 to 2:00 P.M., we will watch a video on customer satisfaction. It will be led by Brad Tailor and it includes quizzes for trainees. The second video is communication skills, and this session will be led by Nina Simon from 3:00 to 4:00 P.M., and it includes networking. That's all.

물론이죠. 먼저 오후 1시부터 2시까지 고객만족에 관한 비디오를 시청하실 것입니다. 그것은 Brad Tailor가 진행할 예정이고, 견습 직원들을 위한 퀴즈를 포함하고 있습니다. 두 번째 비디오는 커뮤니케이션 스킬이며, 이 세션은 오후 3시부터 4시까지 Nina Simon이 진행할 예정이고, 네트워킹을 포함합니다. 이상입니다.

🔊 Is it important for a team leader to have skills for managing conflicts?

팀 리더가 갈등을 해결하는 능력을 갖추는 것이 중요합니까?

IM3   I think it is very important for a team leader to have the skills for managing conflicts. There are two reasons why I think this way.

First, a quick settlement of conflicts will preserve a good atmosphere. A leader should manage the issues quickly to keep the working environment positive.

Second, when conflicts happen at the workplace, a lot of time and energy is wasted on unproductive activities. Thus, every conflict should be addressed instantly.

These are the reasons for my opinion.

저는 팀 리더가 갈등을 해결하는 능력을 갖추는 것이 매우 중요하다고 생각합니다. 제가 이렇게 생각하는 이유는 두 가지입니다.

첫째, 빠른 갈등해결은 좋은 분위기를 유지할 것입니다. 리더는 작업 환경을 긍정적으로 유지하기 위해 문제를 신속하게 처리해야 합니다.

둘째, 직장에서 갈등이 발생할 때, 비생산적인 활동에 많은 시간과 에너지가 낭비됩니다. 그러므로, 모든 갈등은 즉시 해결되어야 합니다.

이것들이 제 의견에 대한 이유입니다.

IH

I think it is very important for a team leader to have the skills for managing conflicts. There are two reasons why I think this way.

First, a quick settlement of conflicts will preserve a good atmosphere. Conflicts form uncomfortable moods. A leader should manage the issues quickly to keep the working environment positive.

Second, when conflicts happen at the workplace, a lot of time and energy is wasted on unproductive activities. Thus, every conflict should be addressed instantly to boost work productivity.

These are the reasons for my opinion.

저는 팀 리더가 갈등을 해결하는 능력을 갖추는 것이 매우 중요하다고 생각합니다. 제가 이렇게 생각하는 이유는 두 가지입니다.

첫째, 빠른 갈등해결은 좋은 분위기를 유지할 것입니다. 갈등은 불편한 기분을 형성합니다. 리더는 작업 환경을 긍정적으로 유지하기 위해 문제를 신속하게 처리해야 합니다.

둘째, 직장에서 갈등이 발생할 때, 비생산적인 활동에 많은 시간과 에너지가 낭비됩니다. 따라서, 모든 갈등은 업무 생산성을 높이기 위해 즉시 해결되어야 합니다.

이것들이 제 의견에 대한 이유입니다.

AL-AH

I think it is very important for a team leader to have the skills for managing conflicts. There are two reasons why I think this way.

First, a quick settlement of conflicts will preserve a good atmosphere. Conflicts form uncomfortable moods. Because it negatively affects work efficiency, a leader should manage the issues quickly to keep the working environment positive.

Second, this skill will save time and energy. When conflicts happen at the workplace, a lot of time and energy is wasted on gossiping and other unproductive activities. Thus, every conflict should be addressed instantly to boost work productivity.

These are the reasons for my opinion.

저는 팀 리더가 갈등을 해결하는 능력을 갖추는 것이 매우 중요하다고 생각합니다. 제가 이렇게 생각하는 이유는 두 가지입니다.

첫째, 빠른 갈등해결은 좋은 분위기를 유지할 것입니다. 갈등은 불편한 기분을 형성합니다. 업무 효율에 부정적인 영향을 미치기 때문에 리더는 업무 환경을 긍정적으로 유지하기 위해 문제를 신속하게 처리해야 합니다.

둘째, 갈등해결 능력은 시간과 에너지를 절약해 줄 것입니다. 직장에서 갈등이 일어날 때, 많은 시간과 에너지가 험담과 다른 비생산적인 활동에 낭비됩니다. 따라서, 모든 갈등은 업무 생산성을 높이기 위해 즉시 해결되어야 합니다.

이것들이 제 의견에 대한 이유입니다.

11

실전유형 모의고사

모범답변·템플릿

Question 1

Hello →/ and welcome back →/ to our Talk Show. ↘// We'll be interviewing a famous rock band, →/ known for their →/ energetic live performances. ↘// The group is made up of →/ a guitarist, ↗/ drummer, ↗/ and singer. ↘// After the interview, →/ they will play a song →/ from the latest release. ↘//

안녕하세요, 저희 토크쇼에 다시 오신 것을 환영합니다. 저희는 활기찬 라이브 공연으로 유명한 록 밴드와 인터뷰를 할 것입니다. 이 그룹은 기타리스트, 드러머, 그리고 보컬로 구성되어 있습니다. 인터뷰가 끝난 후, 그들은 최근에 발매된 곡을 연주할 것입니다.

Question 2

Welcome to the gardening class. ↘// Beginning in a few minutes, →/ the expert gardener →/ Davis Mill will give a talk →/ on designing gardens. ↘// He will talk about designing small gardens, ↗/ the history of garden design, ↗/ and a farmer's life. ↘// Afterward, →/ he will answer any questions →/ you may have. ↘//

정원 가꾸기 수업에 오신 것을 환영합니다. 몇 분 후에, 전문가 정원사 데이비스 밀이 정원 디자인에 대해 강연할 것입니다. 그는 작은 정원을 디자인하는 것, 정원 디자인의 역사, 그리고 농부의 삶에 대해 이야기할 것입니다. 그 후에, 그는 여러분의 질문에 답변해 드릴 예정입니다.

Question 3

| 장소 | This picture was <u>taken at a</u> <u>furniture store</u>. | 이 사진은 가구점에서 찍힌 사진입니다. |

| 중심
대상 | On the right, a woman is <u>handing</u> <u>over the cushion</u> to the other woman. The woman on the left is <u>sitting on the couch</u> and <u>touching</u> <u>the cushion</u>. | 오른쪽에 한 여자가 다른 여자에게 쿠션을 건네주고 있습니다. 왼쪽에 있는 여자는 소파에 앉아 쿠션을 만지고 있습니다. |

| 주변
대상 | In the background, I can see several couches and a chair. | 뒤에 몇 개의 소파와 의자가 보입니다. |

| 상황 | Overall, it seems like they are <u>choosing items</u>. | 전반적으로 그들은 물건을 고르고 있는 것 같습니다. |

Question 4

장소	This picture was <u>taken in the office</u>,	이 사진은 사무실에서 찍은 사진이고,

인원	and a man and a woman are <u>having a meeting</u>.	남자와 여자가 회의를 하고 있습니다.

중심 대상	The man is <u>explaining something important</u>, and the woman is listening to him.	남자는 중요한 것을 설명하고 있고, 여자는 그의 말을 듣고 있습니다.

주변 대상	In the background, another man is working on a computer, and two people are <u>chatting</u>.	후방에는 또 다른 남자가 컴퓨터로 작업을 하고 있고 두 사람이 대화를 하고 있습니다.

🔊 Imagine you're talking on the phone with your friend about having parties.

당신이 친구와 파티를 여는 것에 대해 전화 통화를 한다고 가정해 보세요.

Question 5

Q When was the last time you went to a housewarming party and where was it?

마지막으로 집들이에 간 것은 언제입니까? 파티 장소는 어디였나요?

A The last time I went to a housewarming party was last month and it was held at my friend's place.

제가 마지막으로 집들이에 간 것은 지난 달이었고 친구의 집에서 열렸습니다.

Question 6

Q When you go to a party, do you usually bring a gift for a host?

파티에 갈 때, 보통 초대한 사람에게 줄 선물을 가지고 가시나요?

A Yes, I usually bring a bottle of wine or desserts because I think it's the manner to attend a party.

네, 저는 보통 와인이나 디저트를 가져갑니다. 파티에 참석할 때에 예의라고 생각하기 때문입니다.

Q If you were the host of the party, would you plan activities? Why or why not?

만약 당신이 파티의 주최자라면 당신은 파티에서 뭘 할지를 계획할 것입니까? 그 이유는 무엇인가요?

IM3-IH No, I wouldn't plan activities for the party, and here is why.

First, we can naturally enjoy the party and just relax without any plans.

Second, since everyone has different tastes, it's hard to meet everyone's expectations.

This is why.

아니요, 저는 파티에서 뭘 할지를 계획하지 않을 것이고, 여기 그 이유가 있습니다.

첫째, 우리는 자연스럽게 파티를 즐기고 아무 계획 없이 편안하게 쉴 수 있습니다.

둘째, 사람마다 취향이 다르기 때문에 모두의 기대에 부응하기 어렵습니다.

이것이 그 이유입니다.

AL-AH No, I wouldn't plan activities for the party, and here is why.

First, it's unnecessary. We can naturally enjoy the party and just relax without any plans. A party shouldn't stress people out.

Second, it's unproductive. Since everyone has different tastes in activities, I would never know what kind of activities my guests would like. So, it's hard to meet everyone's expectations. Considering this, I think it would be best to hold the party without any plans.

This is why.

아니요, 저는 파티에서 뭘 할지를 계획하지 않을 것이고, 여기 그 이유가 있습니다.

첫째, 불필요합니다. 우리는 자연스럽게 파티를 즐기고 아무 계획 없이 그냥 쉴 수 있습니다. 파티는 사람들에게 스트레스를 주어서는 안 됩니다.

둘째, 비생산적입니다. 사람마다 활동 취향이 다르기 때문에, 저는 제 손님들이 어떤 활동을 좋아할지 알 수 없을 것입니다. 그래서 모든 사람들의 기대를 충족시키는 것은 어렵습니다. 이런 점을 고려하면 파티는 아무 계획 없이 하는 게 좋을 것 같습니다.

이것이 그 이유입니다.

Professional Development Seminar for Art Teachers
Central Conference Hall, January 15

Time	Session	Speaker
9:00 – 10:00 A.M.	On-site registration	–
10:00 – 11:00 A.M.	Lecture: Preparing students for Art University	Brian Owen
11:00 A.M. - Noon	Workshop: Principles of artful teaching	Johnson Veronica
Noon - 1:00 P.M.	Lunch (Tillet dining hall)	–
1:00 - 2:00 P.M.	Workshop: Developing students as artists	Simon Thomas
2:00 - 3:00 P.M.	Presentation: Virtual art education	Collin Firth

🔊 Hi, can I ask a few questions about the Professional Development Seminar for Art Teachers?

안녕하세요, 미술 선생님들을 위한 전문성 개발 세미나에 대해 몇 가지 질문해도 될까요?

Question 8

Q On what date will the seminar be held and what time will the registration start?

세미나는 며칠에 열리며 등록은 몇 시에 시작되나요?

A The seminar will be held on January 15th and the registration will start at 9:00 A.M.

세미나는 1월 15일에 열리며 등록은 오전 9시에 시작합니다.

Question 9

Q I heard that the lecture on preparing students for Art University will be in the afternoon, correct?

학생들의 예술 대학 입시 준비에 관한 강의가 오후에 있다고 들었는데, 맞나요?

A No, I'm afraid you have the wrong information. The lecture on preparing students for Art University will be in the morning from 10:00 to 11:00 A.M.

아니요, 잘못 아신 것 같습니다. 학생들의 예술 대학 입시 준비에 관한 강의는 오전 10시부터 11시까지 있을 예정입니다.

Question 10

Q Could you give me all the details of the workshops in this seminar?

이번 세미나의 워크숍에 대한 모든 세부 사항을 알려주시겠어요?

A Sure, there are two. The first one is 'Principles of artful teaching', and it will be led by Johnson Veronica from 11:00 A.M. to noon. The second one is 'Developing students as artists', and it will be led by Simon Thomas from 1:00 to 2:00 P.M. That's all.

물론이죠, 두 개 있습니다. 첫 번째 워크숍은 '예술 교육의 원칙'이고, 그것은 오전 11시부터 정오까지 Johnson Veronica가 진행할 것입니다. 두 번째 워크숍은 '학생들을 예술가로 육성 시키기'이고, 오후 1시부터 2시까지 Simon Thomas가 진행할 것입니다. 이상입니다.

🔊 Do you agree or disagree with the following statement?
"It is important to have outdoor playtime during school time."

다음 명제에 동의하십니까, 동의하지 않으십니까?
"학교에서 야외 놀이 시간을 갖는 것은 중요합니다."

IM3　I agree that it is important to have outdoor playtime during school time. I have two reasons.

First, it's an excellent way to relieve stress and relax. These days, students often get stressed from too much schoolwork or extracurricular activities.

Second, they can stay healthy and fit. They need some time for physical activities such as playing sports or taking a walk.

These are the reasons why I agree with the statement.

저는 학교에서 야외 놀이 시간을 갖는 것이 중요하다는 것에 동의합니다. 두 가지 이유가 있습니다.

첫째, 스트레스를 해소하고 휴식을 취할 수 있는 좋은 방법입니다. 요즘, 학생들은 종종 너무 많은 학교 공부나 과외 활동으로 스트레스를 받습니다.

둘째, 그들은 건강하고 활기차게 지낼 수 있습니다. 그들은 스포츠를 하거나 산책을 하는 것과 같은 신체 활동을 위한 시간이 필요합니다.

이것들이 제가 명제에 동의하는 이유입니다.

12

실전유형 모의고사

모범답변·템플릿

IH

I agree that it is important to have outdoor playtime during school time. I have two reasons.

First, it's an excellent way to relieve stress and relax. These days, students often get stressed from too much schoolwork or extracurricular activities. Outdoor playtime will help them focus on their studies and study in a good mood.

Second, they can stay healthy and fit. Since they stay indoors all day at school, they need some time for physical activities such as playing sports or taking a walk.

These are the reasons why I agree with the statement.

저는 학교에서 야외 놀이 시간을 갖는 것이 중요하다는 것에 동의합니다. 두 가지 이유가 있습니다.

첫째, 스트레스를 해소하고 휴식을 취할 수 있는 좋은 방법입니다. 요즘, 학생들은 종종 너무 많은 학교 공부나 과외 활동으로 스트레스를 받습니다. 야외 놀이 시간은 그들이 공부에 집중하고 기분 좋게 공부하도록 도와줄 것입니다.

둘째, 그들은 건강하고 활기차게 지낼 수 있습니다. 그들은 학교에서 하루 종일 실내에 있기 때문에, 스포츠를 하거나 산책을 하는 것과 같은 신체 활동을 위한 시간이 필요합니다.

이것들이 제가 명제에 동의하는 이유입니다.

AL-AH

I agree that it is important to have outdoor playtime during school time. I have two reasons.

First, it's an excellent way to relieve stress and relax. These days, students often get stressed from too much schoolwork or extracurricular activities. They need some refreshments. Considering this, outdoor playtime will help them focus on their studies and study in a good mood.

Second, they can stay healthy and fit. Since they stay indoors all day at school, they need some time for physical activities such as playing sports or taking a walk. This will improve their physical and mental health.

These are the reasons why I agree with the statement.

저는 학교에서 야외 놀이 시간을 갖는 것이 중요하다는 것에 동의합니다. 두 가지 이유가 있습니다.

첫째, 스트레스를 해소하고 휴식을 취할 수 있는 좋은 방법입니다. 요즘, 학생들은 종종 너무 많은 학교 공부나 과외 활동으로 스트레스를 받습니다. 그들은 재충전이 필요합니다. 이것을 고려하면, 야외 놀이 시간은 그들이 공부에 집중하고 기분 좋게 공부하는 데 도움이 될 것입니다.

둘째, 그들은 건강하고 활기차게 지낼 수 있습니다. 그들은 학교에서 하루 종일 실내에 있기 때문에, 스포츠를 하거나 산책을 하는 것과 같은 신체 활동을 위한 시간이 필요합니다. 이것은 그들의 신체적, 정신적 건강을 향상시킬 것입니다.

이것들이 제가 명제에 동의하는 이유입니다.

Question 1

Welcome to Peter's Park. ↘// On today's tour, →/ we will walk through →/ a beautiful collection →/ of plants and flowers. ↘// Through the property, →/ you'll see →/ many varieties of daisies, ↗/ roses, ↗/ and tulips. ↘// While enjoying the tour, →/ please feel free →/ to take photographs. ↘//

Peter's Park에 오신 것을 환영합니다. 오늘 투어에서는 아름다운 식물과 꽃 컬렉션을 둘러볼 것입니다. 그곳에서 여러분은 다양한 종류의 데이지, 장미, 튤립을 보실 수 있습니다. 투어를 즐기시는 동안, 자유롭게 사진 촬영이 가능합니다.

Question 2

We're thrilled to announce →/ the grand opening →/ of a new bar →/ in Frankland city. ↘// Though everyone can find →/ what they like, →/ the Whitehouse is →/ mainly a wine bar. ↘// The menu includes →/ cheese boards, ↗/ salmon pasta, ↗/ and grilled chicken. ↘// What's more, →/ we have a fantastic children's menu. ↘// Make your reservation today. ↘//

Frankland시에 있는 새로운 바의 개점을 알리게 되어 기쁩니다. 누구나 좋아할 만한 메뉴들이 있지만, Whitehouse는 주로 와인 바입니다. 메뉴에는 모둠 치즈, 연어 파스타, 구운 닭고기가 포함되어 있습니다. 게다가, 훌륭한 어린이 메뉴도 있습니다. 오늘 예약하세요.

장소	This picture was <u>taken on the street</u>.	이 사진은 거리에서 찍힌 사진입니다.

중심 대상	What I notice first is two red buses <u>running on the road</u>. On each side, many <u>pedestrians are walking by</u>.	맨 처음 눈에 띄는 것은 도로를 달리고 있는 두 대의 빨간 버스입니다. 양쪽에는 많은 보행자들이 지나가고 있습니다.

주변 대상	Also, there are many buildings, stores, and trees along the street.	또한 길을 따라 많은 건물, 가게, 나무들이 있습니다.

상황	Overall, this place seems <u>quite busy and crowded</u>.	전반적으로 이곳은 꽤 바쁘고 붐비는 것 같습니다.

Question 4

| 장소 | This picture was <u>taken on the street</u>. | 이 사진은 거리에서 찍힌 사진입니다. |

| 중심 대상 | In this picture, two men are <u>walking on the path</u>. They are <u>showing their backs</u> to the camera, and the man on the left is <u>carrying a guitar on his shoulder</u>. | 사진 속 두 남자는 길을 걷고 있습니다. 그들은 카메라를 등 지고 서 있고, 왼쪽에 있는 남자는 어깨에 기타를 메고 있습니다. |

| 주변 대상 | In the background, there are trees <u>planted in a row</u>, and many cars are <u>parked along the street</u>. | 배경에는 나무들이 일렬로 심어져 있고, 길가에 많은 차가 주차되어 있습니다. |

🔊 Imagine you are having a telephone interview with a magazine publisher about work.

일에 대해 잡지사와 전화 인터뷰를 한다고 가정해 보세요.

Question 5

Q What do you do for work, or if you're a student, what do you study?

무슨 일을 하고 있나요, 학생이라면 무엇을 공부를 하고 있나요?

A I am an office worker and I work for a marketing company. I've been working here for five years and I am satisfied with my job.

저는 회사원이고 마케팅 회사에서 일하고 있습니다. 저는 이곳에서 5년 동안 일했고, 제 일에 만족합니다.

Question 6

Q Do you think the location of a company is important? Why or why not?

회사의 위치가 중요하다고 생각합니까? 이유는 무엇인가요?

A Yes, it's crucial and critical. A long commute makes me exhausted. Also, it's time consuming.

네, 그것은 중대하고 중요합니다. 장거리 통근은 저를 지치게 합니다.
또한, 시간이 많이 걸립니다.

Q Which of the following is the most important factor when getting a job?

- Opportunities for promotion
- Good employee benefits
- The availability of a flexible schedule

다음 중 취업할 때 가장 중요하게 고려해야 할 사항은 무엇입니까?

- 승진 기회
- 좋은 직원 복지
- 탄력근무제 가능 여부

`IM3-IH` For me, the most important factor when getting a job is the availability of a flexible schedule, and here is why.

First, I can work with personal commitments such as childcare or self-development.

Second, it increases work productivity because I can work when I can focus better.

This is why.

저에게 있어 취업할 때 가장 중요하게 고려해야 할 것은 탄력근무제 가능 여부이며, 여기 그 이유가 있습니다.

첫째, 육아나 자기 계발 같은 개인적인 일을 할 수 있습니다.

둘째, 집중을 잘할 수 있을 때 일을 할 수 있기 때문에 업무 생산성을 높입니다.

이것이 그 이유입니다.

`AL-AH` For me, the most important factor when getting a job is the availability of a flexible schedule, and here is why.

First, it allows me to work with personal commitments such as childcare, self-development, or leisure activities.

Second, it increases work productivity. For instance, when I work during my peak productivity hours, I can get more work done in less time.

This is why.

저에게 있어 취업할 때 가장 중요하게 고려해야 할 것은 탄력근무제 가능 여부이며, 여기 그 이유가 있습니다.

첫째, 육아, 자기 계발, 여가 활동과 같은 개인적인 약속을 가지고 일할 수 있게 해줍니다.

둘째, 업무 생산성을 높입니다. 예를 들어 생산성이 가장 높은 시간에 일할 때 더 적은 시간에 더 많은 작업을 수행할 수 있습니다.

이것이 그 이유입니다.

Genie's Art Classes

Santa Ana art center: Main classroom, Fall semester: October 3 - November 2
Fee: membership 20$, non-membership 30$

Pencil drawing	Mondays	9:00 - 10:00 A.M.
Draw and sketch	Tuesdays	10:00 - 11:00 A.M.
Digital sketching for beginners	Tuesdays	11:00 A.M. - Noon
Watercolor painting for beginners	Wednesdays	2:00 - 3:30 P.M.
Figure drawing	Fridays	1:00 - 2:00 P.M.
Sculpture	Saturdays	7:30 - 9:30 P.M.

🔊 Hi, can I ask a few questions about the fall semester of Genie's Art Classes?

안녕하세요, Genie's Art Classes의 가을 학기에 대해 몇 가지 여쭤봐도 될까요?

Question 8

Q On what date will the fall semester begin and in what room will the classes be?

가을 학기는 며칠에 시작하며 어떤 강의실에서 열리나요?

A The fall semester will begin on October 3rd, and the classes will be in the main classroom of the Santa Ana art center.

가을 학기는 10월 3일에 시작되며, 수업은 산타 아나 아트 센터의 메인 클래스룸에서 진행됩니다.

Question 9

Q I heard that the class costs 15 dollars for art center members. Could you confirm it?

아트 센터 회원은 강의 비용이 15달러라고 들었습니다. 확인해 주시겠어요?

A Well, I am afraid you have the wrong information. It's 20 dollars per class for art center members.

잘못 알고 계신 것 같습니다. 아트센터 회원은 한 강의 당 20달러입니다.

Question 10

Q I can take a class on Wednesdays and Saturdays. Could you give me all the details of the classes on Wednesdays and Saturdays?

저는 수요일과 토요일에 수업을 들을 수 있어요. 수요일과 토요일 수업에 대한 모든 세부 사항을 알려주시겠어요?

A Sure, there are two. The first one is 'Watercolor painting for beginners' and it will be on Wednesdays from 2:00 to 3:30 P.M. The second one is 'Sculpture' and it will be on Saturdays from 7:30 to 9:30 P.M. That's all.

물론입니다, 두 개의 강의가 있습니다. 첫 번째는 '초보자를 위한 수채화' 강의이며 수요일 오후 2시부터 3시 30분까지입니다. 두 번째는 '조각'이고 토요일 저녁 7시 30분부터 9시 30분까지입니다. 이상입니다.

🔊 Do you agree or disagree with the following statement?
"It is necessary for teachers to attend training workshops each year."

다음 명제에 동의하십니까, 동의하지 않으십니까?
"교사들은 매년 교육 워크숍에 참석해야 합니다."

IM3 I agree that it is necessary for teachers to attend training workshops each year. There are two reasons why I think this way.

First, teachers need proper teaching skills not to fall behind. Also, teachers should keep up with the changes.

Second, it will enhance their teaching techniques. To be effective, teachers should learn how to manage online educational programs.

These are the reasons why I agree with this.

저는 선생님들이 매년 교육 워크숍에 참석하는 것이 필요하다는 것에 동의합니다. 제가 이렇게 생각하는 이유는 두 가지입니다.

첫째, 선생님들은 뒤처지지 않기 위해 적절한 교육 기술이 필요합니다. 또한, 선생님들은 변화를 따라가야 합니다.

둘째, 그것은 그들의 교수법을 향상시킬 것입니다. 효과적이기 위해서, 선생님들은 온라인 교육 프로그램을 관리하는 방법을 배워야 합니다.

이것들이 제가 명제에 동의하는 이유입니다.

IH

I agree that it is necessary for teachers to attend training workshops each year. There are two reasons why I think this way.

First, teachers need proper teaching skills not to fall behind. Also, they should keep up with the changes and adapt to new things well.

Second, it will enhance their teaching techniques. To be effective, teachers should learn how to manage online educational programs or resources in a more efficient way.

These are the reasons why I agree with this.

저는 선생님들이 매년 교육 워크숍에 참석하는 것이 필요하다는 것에 동의합니다. 제가 이렇게 생각하는 이유는 두 가지입니다.

첫째, 선생님들은 뒤처지지 않기 위해 적절한 교육 기술이 필요합니다. 또한, 그들은 변화를 따라가야 하고 새로운 것에 잘 적응해야 합니다.

둘째, 그것은 그들의 교수법을 향상시킬 것입니다. 효과적이기 위해서, 선생님들은 온라인 교육 프로그램이나 자원을 더 효율적인 방법으로 관리하는 방법을 배워야 합니다.

이것들이 제가 명제에 동의하는 이유입니다.

AL-AH

I agree that it is necessary for teachers to attend training workshops each year. There are two reasons why I think this way.

First, teachers need proper teaching skills not to fall behind. For example, things change very fast in modern society. So, they should keep up with the changes and adapt to new things well.

Second, it will enhance their teaching techniques. For instance, the younger generation study electronically. So, to be effective, teachers should learn how to manage online educational programs or resources in a more efficient way.

These are the reasons why I agree with this.

저는 선생님들이 매년 교육 워크숍에 참석하는 것이 필요하다는 것에 동의합니다. 제가 이렇게 생각하는 이유는 두 가지입니다.

첫째, 선생님들은 뒤처지지 않기 위해 적절한 교육 기술이 필요합니다. 예를 들어, 현대 사회에서는 상황이 매우 빠르게 변합니다. 그래서, 그들은 변화를 따라가야 하고 새로운 것들에 잘 적응해야 합니다.

둘째, 그것은 그들의 교수법을 향상시킬 것입니다. 예를 들어, 젊은 세대들은 전자적으로 (컴퓨터로) 공부합니다. 그래서, 효과적이기 위해서, 선생님들은 온라인 교육 프로그램이나 자원을 더 효율적인 방법으로 관리하는 방법을 배워야 합니다.

이것들이 제가 명제에 동의하는 이유입니다.

13

실전유형 모의고사

모범답변·템플릿

Question 1

Welcome to →/ Channel Twelve weather news. ↘// The snow →/ that started yesterday →/ will continue →/ throughout the day. ↘// Sunday, →/ however, →/ conditions will improve →/ with warmer temperatures, ↗/ clear skies, ↗/ and a light breeze. ↘// If you are interested in →/ how today's weather affects traffic, →/ stay tuned, →/ because the traffic news →/ is next. ↘//

채널 12 일기 예보에 오신 것을 환영합니다. 어제부터 내린 눈은 하루 종일 이어지겠습니다. 하지만 일요일에는 기온이 더 올라가고, 하늘이 맑아지며, 바람은 약해지겠습니다. 만약 오늘의 날씨가 교통 상황에 어떤 영향을 미치는지 궁금하시다면, 다음으로 교통 뉴스가 이어지니 채널을 고정하세요.

Question 2

Thank you for attending →/ this writing seminar. ↘// Today, →/ we will start with a workshop →/ led by Erick Sharon, →/ a writing instructor at the local community center. ↘// Mr. Sharon is also →/ a famous writer. ↘// His third fiction →/ Red Night →/ has just been published →/ this year. ↘// During the workshop, →/ he'll be discussing →/ how to develop →/ fiction elements of plot, ↗/ setting, ↗/ character, ↗/ and conflict. ↘//

글쓰기 세미나에 참석해 주셔서 감사합니다. 오늘은 지역 주민센터의 글쓰기 강사 Erick Sharon이 이끄는 워크숍으로 시작하겠습니다. 또한 Sharon씨는 유명한 작가입니다. 그의 세 번째 소설인 레드 나이트가 올해 막 출판되었습니다. 워크숍에서 그는 줄거리, 배경, 인물, 갈등의 소설 요소를 어떻게 발전시킬지에 대해 얘기할 것입니다.

Question 3

장소	This picture was <u>taken at an outdoor restaurant</u>.	이 사진은 야외 식당에서 찍혔습니다.

인원	There are several people in the scene.	이 장면에는 여러 사람들이 있습니다.

중심 대상	In the center, a female customer is <u>sitting at the table</u> while <u>making an order</u>, and a waiter is <u>taking an order from her</u>.	중앙에는 한 여성 고객이 테이블에 앉아 주문을 하고 있고 한 종업원은 그녀로부터 주문을 받고 있습니다.

주변 대상	In the background, I can see more employees and customers.	배경에는 더 많은 직원들과 고객들이 보입니다.

상황	Overall, it seems like people are <u>enjoying meals</u> on a beautiful sunny day.	전반적으로 아름답고 화창한 날에 사람들이 식사를 즐기고 있는 것처럼 보입니다.

Question 4

장소	This picture was <u>taken at a pottery class</u>.	이 사진은 도자기 수업에서 찍힌 사진입니다.
중심대상	On the right, a teacher is <u>giving a demonstration</u> on how to make a vase, and the others are <u>paying attention</u>. One of the attendees is <u>pointing at the vase and asking a question</u>.	오른쪽에는 선생님이 꽃병 만드는 법을 시연하고 있고, 다른 사람들은 집중하고 있습니다. 참석자 중 한 명이 꽃병을 가리키며 질문을 하고 있습니다.
주변대상	In the background, I can see some boxes and shelves.	뒤에는 상자와 선반이 보입니다.
상황	Overall, it seems like they are focusing.	전반적으로 그들은 집중하고 있는 듯 보입니다.

Question 5

Q Who does most of the cleaning of your room, and why?

당신의 방을 가장 많이 청소를 하는 사람은 누구이며, 그 이유는 무엇입니까?

A I am the only one who cleans my room because I live alone. There is no one to clean my place except for me.

저는 혼자 살기 때문에 방 청소는 제가 합니다. 저 말고는 방을 청소할 사람이 없습니다.

Question 6

Q Do you spend more time cleaning your room than you did five years ago? Why or why not?

당신은 5년 전보다 당신의 방을 청소하는 데 더 많은 시간을 보내나요? 왜 그런가요? 혹은 왜 그렇지 않은가요?

A No, I spend the same time cleaning my room as I did in the past. Nothing has changed with it.

아니요, 저는 제 방을 청소하는 데 예전과 같은 시간을 보냅니다. 아무것도 변한 게 없어요.

Q If you clean your room, would you start with the easiest task or with the most difficult one, and why?

만약 당신이 당신의 방을 청소한다면 당신은 가장 쉬운 일부터 시작할 것인가요, 아니면 가장 어려운 일부터 시작할 것인가요? 그리고 그 이유는 무엇인가요?

`IM3-IH` In that case, I will start with the easiest task, and here is why.

First, if I start with the most difficult task, I may get stressed out.

Second, if I start with the easiest thing, I can clean up step-by-step and finish cleaning easily.

This is why.

그러한 경우에 저는 가장 쉬운 일부터 시작할 것이고, 여기 그 이유가 있습니다.

첫째, 가장 어려운 일부터 시작하면 스트레스를 받을 수도 있습니다.

둘째, 가장 쉬운 것부터 시작하면 단계별로 청소를 할 수 있고 청소를 쉽게 끝낼 수 있습니다.

이것이 그 이유입니다.

`AL-AH` In that case, I will start with the easiest task, and here is why.

First, if I start with the most difficult task, I may get stressed out and give up cleaning itself.

Second, if I start with the easiest thing, I can clean up step-by-step and finish even the difficult tasks naturally. This is a much more productive and easier way to finish cleaning.

This is why.

그러한 경우에 저는 가장 쉬운 일부터 시작할 것이고, 여기 그 이유가 있습니다.

첫째, 가장 어려운 일부터 시작하면 스트레스를 받아 청소 자체를 포기할 수도 있습니다.

둘째, 가장 쉬운 것부터 시작하면 단계별로 청소를 할 수 있고 어려운 일도 자연스럽게 마무리할 수 있습니다. 이것이 청소를 끝내는 훨씬 더 생산적이고 쉬운 방법입니다.

이것이 그 이유입니다.

Library Management Conference
Hiller's hall, room 201, October 3

Schedule	
9:00 - 10:00 A.M.	President's speech
10:00 - 11:00 A.M.	Lecture: qualified librarians
11:00 A.M. - Noon	Workshop: management of children's book section
Noon - 1:00 P.M.	Buffet lunch
1:00 - 2:00 P.M.	Group discussion: films for children
2:00 - 3:00 P.M.	Presentation: issues with old books
3:00 - 4:00 P.M.	Award ceremony: best librarians of this year

🔊 Hi, I hope you could give me some information about the library management conference.

안녕하세요, 도서관 경영 회의에 대해 정보를 좀 주셨으면 합니다.

Question 8

Q Where will the conference be held, and what is the first session of it?

회의는 어디에서 열리며, 첫 번째 세션은 무엇입니까?

A The conference will be held in room 201 at Hiller's hall and its first session is the president's speech from 9:00 to 10:00 A.M.

회의는 힐러 홀 201호에서 열리며 첫 번째 세션은 오전 9시부터 10시까지 진행되는 회장님의 연설입니다.

Question 9

Q I heard that the award ceremony will be in the morning, correct?

시상식이 오전에 진행된다고 들었습니다. 맞나요?

A No, the award ceremony will be in the afternoon from 3:00 to 4:00 P.M. Please keep that in mind.

아니요, 시상식은 오후 3시부터 4시까지입니다. 이 점을 명심해 주세요.

Question 10

Q Could you give me all the details of the sessions that will deal with children-related issues?

어린이와 관련된 주제를 다루는 세션의 모든 세부 사항을 알려주시겠어요?

A Sure, there are two. The first one is a workshop on management of children's book section and it will be from 11:00 A.M. to noon.
The second one is a group discussion on films for children and it will be from 1:00 to 2:00 P.M. That's all.

네, 두 개 있습니다. 첫 번째는 아동 도서 부문 경영에 대한 워크숍이고 오전 11시부터 정오까지 진행될 예정입니다. 두 번째 세션은 어린이를 위한 영화에 대한 단체 토론이며 오후 1시부터 2시까지 진행될 예정입니다. 이상입니다.

🔊 Which is more important for a salesperson's success: having social skills or having extensive knowledge of the products being sold?

판매원의 성공을 위해 사회성을 갖추는 것과 판매 중인 제품에 대한 광범위한 지식을 갖추는 것 중 어느 것이 더 중요합니까?

IM3   I think having social skills is more important when it comes to the salesperson's success. There are two reasons for this.

First, it's crucial and critical. Their nice attitude gives us pleasant experiences. The customers would be more willing to buy products from the kind salesperson.

Second, people already know a lot about the products they are considering buying because we have YouTube and other useful websites.

These are the reasons.

저는 판매원의 성공을 위해서는 사회성을 갖추는 것이 더 중요하다고 생각합니다. 여기에는 두 가지 이유가 있습니다.

첫째, 중요하고 중대합니다. 그들의 좋은 태도는 우리에게 즐거운 경험을 줍니다. 고객들은 친절한 판매원으로부터 제품을 더 많이 구매할 것입니다.

둘째, 사람들은 이미 유튜브와 다른 유용한 웹사이트들이 있기 때문에 그들이 구매를 고려하고 있는 제품에 대해 많이 알고 있습니다.

이것들이 그 이유입니다.

IH

I think having social skills is more important when it comes to the salesperson's success. There are two reasons for this.

First, it's crucial and critical. Friendly people and <u>their nice attitude give us pleasant experiences</u>. So, the customers would be more willing to buy products from the kind salesperson because they are treated in a good way.

Second, <u>people already know a lot about the products they are considering buying</u> because we have YouTube and other useful websites. So, extensive knowledge is not an effective trigger for sales.

These are the reasons.

저는 판매원의 성공을 위해서는 사회성을 갖추는 것이 더 중요하다고 생각합니다. 여기에는 두 가지 이유가 있습니다.

첫째, 중요하고 중대합니다. 친절한 사람들과 그들의 좋은 태도는 우리에게 즐거운 경험을 줍니다. 따라서, 고객들은 친절한 판매원에게 좋은 대우를 받기 때문에 물건을 구매할 의향이 더 있을 것입니다.

둘째, 사람들은 이미 유튜브와 다른 유용한 웹사이트들이 있기 때문에 그들이 구매를 고려하고 있는 제품에 대해 많이 알고 있습니다. 따라서 광범위한 지식은 효과적인 판매촉진이 되지 못합니다.

이것들이 그 이유입니다.

AL-AH

I think having social skill is more important when it comes to the salesperson's success. There are two reasons for this.

First, it's crucial and critical. For example, good customer service makes people feel better. Friendly people and <u>their nice attitude give us pleasant experiences</u>. So, the customers would be more willing to buy products from the kind salesperson because they are treated in a good way.

Second, <u>people already know a lot about the products they are considering buying</u> because we have YouTube and other useful websites. Also, too much information about the product might be confusing. So, extensive knowledge is not an effective trigger for sales.

These are the reasons.

저는 판매원의 성공을 위해서는 사회성을 갖추는 것이 더 중요하다고 생각합니다. 여기에는 두 가지 이유가 있습니다.

첫째, 중요하고 중대합니다. 예를 들어, 좋은 고객 서비스는 사람들의 기분을 좋게 해줍니다. 친절한 사람들과 그들의 좋은 태도는 우리에게 즐거운 경험을 줍니다. 따라서, 고객들은 친절한 판매원에게 좋은 대우를 받기 때문에 물건을 구매할 의향이 더 있을 것입니다.

둘째, 사람들은 이미 유튜브와 다른 유용한 웹사이트들이 있기 때문에 그들이 구매를 고려하고 있는 제품에 대해 많이 알고 있습니다. 또한 제품에 대한 정보가 너무 많으면 혼란스러울 수 있습니다. 따라서 광범위한 지식은 효과적인 판매촉진이 되지 못합니다.

이것들이 그 이유입니다.

14 실전유형 모의고사

모범답변·템플릿

Question 1

If you are looking for →/ summer activities →/ for your teenagers, →/ check out Park Hill community center. ↘// This summer, →/ Park Hill community center →/ will offer programs →/ in volunteering, ↗/ media, ↗/ and career. ↘// These programs are →/ specifically designed for teenagers →/ and will be able to accommodate →/ any skill level. ↘// For more information →/ on programs, please visit our website. ↘//

당신의 십 대 자녀들을 위한 여름 활동을 찾고 있다면, 파크 힐 주민 센터를 확인해 보세요. 올여름, 파크 힐 주민 센터는 자원봉사, 미디어, 그리고 직업에 관한 프로그램을 제공할 예정입니다. 이 프로그램들은 특별히 십 대들을 대상으로 하고 있으며 어떤 수준의 학생도 들을 수 있습니다. 프로그램에 대한 자세한 내용은 웹 사이트를 방문해 주세요.

Question 2

Attention, →/ passengers. ↘// This is the express bus →/ to Albertson Ville. ↘// Please note →/ that we're not going to stop →/ at Billington station, →/ which is currently under construction. ↘// Before you exit the bus, →/ please make sure →/ to take any bags, ↗/ small electronic devices, ↗/ and other personal belongings. ↘// Thank you for traveling with us today. ↘//

승객 여러분, 주목해 주세요. 이 버스는 Albertson Ville로 가는 고속버스입니다. 현재 공사 중인 Billington 역은 정차하지 않습니다. 버스에서 내리시기 전에 가방, 소형 전자기기, 기타 개인 소지품을 꼭 챙기시기 바랍니다. 오늘 저희 버스를 이용해 주셔서 감사합니다.

장소	This picture was taken at a park.	이 사진은 공원에서 찍힌 사진입니다.
인원	Three students are sitting on the ground.	세 명의 학생이 땅에 앉아 있습니다.
중심 대상	The man on the left is about to open his laptop. The man in the center is taking out something from his backpack. The woman on the right is trying to open her notebook.	왼쪽에 있는 남자가 그의 노트북을 열려고 합니다. 중앙에 있는 남자는 배낭에서 무언가를 꺼내고 있습니다. 오른쪽에 있는 여성은 그녀의 공책을 펼치려고 합니다.
상황	It seems that they are getting ready to study.	그들은 공부할 준비를 하는 듯 보입니다.

Question 4

장소	This picture was <u>taken in the kitchen</u>.	이 사진은 부엌에서 찍힌 사진입니다.

인원	Two cleaners are working.	청소부 두 명이 일하고 있습니다.

중심 대상	The woman on the right is <u>cleaning the window with a duster</u>. The other woman is <u>wiping the sink</u> with a dishrag. They are wearing yellow uniforms.	오른쪽에 있는 여성은 먼지떨이로 창문을 청소하고 있습니다. 다른 여자는 행주로 싱크대를 닦고 있습니다. 그들은 노란색 유니폼을 입고 있습니다.

주변 대상	Also, I can see a few houses through the window.	또한, 창문 너머로 몇 채의 집들이 보입니다.

상황	Overall, this place seems <u>tidy</u>.	전반적으로 이곳은 깔끔해 보입니다.

🔊 Imagine a travel magazine publisher is conducting research about traveling. You have agreed to participate in a telephone interview about it.

여행 잡지사에서 여행에 대한 연구를 수행하고 있다고 가정해 보십시오. 당신은 이와 관련된 전화 인터뷰에 참여하기로 동의했습니다.

Question 5

Q Do you like to read travel articles? Why or why not?

여행 기사를 읽는 것을 좋아하세요? 그 이유는 무엇입니까?

A I don't like to read travel articles. Instead, I prefer to watch travel videos on YouTube.

여행 기사를 읽는 것을 좋아하지 않습니다. 대신 유튜브를 통해 여행 비디오를 보는 것을 선호합니다.

Question 6

Q When was the last time you traveled abroad, and who did you travel with?

마지막으로 언제 해외여행을 다녀오셨나요, 그리고 누구와 함께 갔습니까?

A The last time I traveled abroad was 2 years ago, and I traveled with my family.

마지막으로 해외여행을 다녀온 것은 2년 전이며, 가족과 함께 다녀왔습니다.

Q When traveling abroad, do you prefer to travel throughout the countryside or the city?

해외여행을 할 때 당신은 시골 여행과 도시 여행 중 무엇을 선호하나요?

IM3-IH In that case, I prefer to travel throughout the countryside, and here is why.

First, I can enjoy the beautiful scenery, such as mountains, forests, and beaches.

Second, I can do outdoor activities like hiking, camping, fishing, and so forth.

This is why.

그러한 경우에 저는 시골을 여행하는 것을 선호하는데, 여기 그 이유가 있습니다.

첫째, 저는 산, 숲, 그리고 해변과 같은 아름다운 경치를 즐길 수 있습니다.

둘째, 하이킹, 캠핑, 낚시 등 야외 활동을 할 수 있습니다.

이것이 그 이유입니다.

AL-AH In that case, I prefer to travel throughout the countryside, and here is why.

First, I can enjoy the beautiful scenery. For example, the countryside offers admirable natural landscapes such as mountains, forests, and beaches. This could be a relaxing escape from the city.

Second, there are adventurous outdoor activities available, like hiking, camping, fishing, and so forth. This will refresh my mind and relieve my stress.

This is why.

그러한 경우에 저는 시골을 여행하는 것을 선호하는데, 여기 그 이유가 있습니다.

첫째, 저는 아름다운 경치를 즐길 수 있습니다. 예를 들어 시골에는 산, 숲, 그리고 해변과 같은 훌륭한 자연 경관이 있습니다. 그래서 여유롭게 잠시 도시를 벗어날 수 있습니다.

둘째, 하이킹, 캠핑, 낚시 등과 같은 모험적인 야외 활동이 가능합니다. 그래서 저는 기분전환을 하고 스트레스를 풀 것입니다.

이것이 그 이유입니다.

Palm State University
George Stephan, President, December 2

9:00 - 10:00 A.M.	President's speech
10:00 - 11:00 A.M.	Presentation: Career and further studies
11:00 A.M. - Noon	Committee meeting: Academic affairs, Room 12
Noon - 1:00 P.M.	Lunch (Phillip Kim, vice president)
1:00 - 2:00 P.M.	Lecture: International law class
2:00 - 3:00 P.M.	Committee meeting: Finance, Conference room A
3:00 - 4:00 P.M.	Social hour: Student-award recipients

🔊 Hi, this is George Stephan, the president of Palm State University. I have a few questions about my schedule on December 2nd.

안녕하세요, 저는 팜 주립 대학의 총장인 조지 스테판입니다.
12월 2일 제 일정에 대한 몇 가지 질문이 있습니다.

Question 8

Q What is the last item of my schedule, and what time does it end?

제 일정의 마지막 세션은 무엇이며, 그것은 몇 시에 끝납니까?

A The last item of your schedule is 'social hour' with student-award recipients and it ends at 4:00 P.M.

당신의 일정의 마지막 세션은 학생상 수상자들과 함께하는 '사교 시간'이며, 그것은 오후 4시에 끝납니다.

Question 9

Q I remember that the 'International law class' will be before lunch. Is that correct?

저는 '국제법 수업'이 점심 식사 전에 있는 것으로 기억하고 있습니다. 그것이 맞습니까?

A No, the 'International law class' will take place after lunch from 1:00 to 2:00 P.M.

아닙니다, '국제법 수업'은 점심 식사 후 오후 1시부터 2시까지 진행됩니다.

Question 10

Q I know that I will have committee meetings. Could you give me all the details of the committee meetings?

위원회 회의가 있다고 알고 있습니다. 위원회 회의에 대한 모든 세부 사항을 알려주시겠어요?

A Sure, there are two. The first one will be from 11:00 A.M. to noon in room twelve, and we will discuss academic affairs. The second one will be from 2:00 to 3:00 P.M. in conference room A and finance issues will be discussed.

물론이죠, 두 개 있습니다. 첫 번째 회의는 오전 11시부터 정오까지 12호실에서 학업에 대해 논의할 것입니다. 두 번째 회의는 오후 2시부터 3시까지 A 회의실에서 진행될 예정이며 재정 관련 사항이 논의될 것입니다.

🔊 Do you agree or disagree with the following statement?
"Reading a book relaxes you more than exercising."

다음 명제에 동의하십니까, 동의하지 않으십니까?
"운동보다 독서가 당신을 더 편하게 해줍니다."

IM3 I agree that reading a book relaxes you more than exercising. There are two reasons why I think in this way.

First, it calms us down. For example, we can take a mental break.

Second, exercising is often tiring and demanding. For instance, we need to make lots of movements and keep concentrating on working out in the right way.

These are the reasons why I agree that reading a book relaxes you more than exercising.

저는 운동보다 독서가 당신을 더 편안하게 한다는 것에 동의합니다. 제가 이렇게 생각하는 이유는 두 가지입니다.

첫째, 그것은 우리를 차분하게 만듭니다. 예를 들어, 우리는 정신적인 휴식을 취할 수 있습니다.

둘째, 운동은 종종 피곤하고 힘든 일입니다. 예를 들어, 우리는 많이 움직여야 하고 올바른 방법으로 운동하는 데 계속 집중해야 합니다.

이것들이 제가 운동보다 독서가 당신을 더 편안하게 해준다는 것에 동의하는 이유입니다.

IH I agree that reading a book relaxes you more than exercising. There are two reasons why I think in this way.

First, it calms us down. For example, <u>we can take a mental break</u> and escape from our routines while reading.

Second, <u>exercising is often tiring and demanding</u>. For instance, we need to make lots of movements and keep concentrating on working out in the right way. These activities often make us physically exhausted.

These are the reasons why I agree that reading a book relaxes you more than exercising.

저는 운동보다 독서가 당신을 더 편안하게 한다는 것에 동의합니다. 제가 이렇게 생각하는 이유는 두 가지입니다.

첫째, 그것은 우리를 차분하게 만듭니다. 예를 들어, 우리는 독서를 하는 동안 정신적인 휴식을 취하고 일상에서 벗어날 수 있습니다.

둘째, 운동은 종종 피곤하고 힘든 일입니다. 예를 들어, 우리는 많이 움직여야 하고 올바른 방법으로 운동하는 데 계속 집중해야 합니다. 이러한 활동들은 종종 우리를 육체적으로 지치게 만듭니다.

이것들이 제가 운동보다 독서가 당신을 더 편안하게 해준다는 것에 동의하는 이유입니다.

AL-AH I agree that reading a book relaxes you more than exercising. There are two reasons why I think in this way.

First, it calms us down. For example, <u>we can take a mental break</u> and escape from our routines while reading. So, it's an excellent way to relieve stress and ease tension.

Second, <u>exercising is often tiring and demanding</u>. For instance, we need to make lots of movements and keep concentrating on working out in the right way. These activities often make us physically exhausted. Although we can stay fit by exercising, I would say it's refreshing rather than relaxing.

These are the reasons why I agree that reading a book relaxes you more than exercising.

저는 운동보다 독서가 당신을 더 편안하게 한다는 것에 동의합니다. 제가 이렇게 생각하는 이유는 두 가지입니다.

첫째, 그것은 우리를 차분하게 만듭니다. 예를 들어, 우리는 독서를 하는 동안 정신적인 휴식을 취하고 일상에서 벗어날 수 있습니다. 그래서, 독서는 스트레스를 해소하고 긴장을 완화하는 훌륭한 방법입니다.

둘째, 운동은 종종 피곤하고 힘든 일입니다. 예를 들어, 우리는 많이 움직여야 하고 올바른 방법으로 운동하는 데 계속 집중해야 합니다. 이러한 활동들은 종종 우리를 육체적으로 지치게 만듭니다. 비록 우리가 운동을 함으로써 건강을 유지할 수 있지만, 저는 운동이 긴장을 푸는 것보다 기분 전환을 해준다고 말하고 싶습니다.

이것들이 제가 운동보다 독서가 당신을 더 편안하게 해준다는 것에 동의하는 이유입니다.

15

실전유형 모의고사

모범답변·템플릿

Question 1

Welcome to the guided tour. ↘// You are now →/ at the main gallery →/ of the British Museum. ↘// In front of you →/ is a replica of a plane, →/ Brave Lion, →/ built forty years ago, →/ and this small airplane →/ was designed by →/ Peter Strokes. ↘// This plane has →/ a relatively small wingspan, ↗/ two-hundred-gallon fuel capacity, ↗/ and seating for five passengers. ↘//

가이드 투어에 오신 것을 환영합니다. 여러분은 지금 대영박물관의 메인 갤러리에 있습니다. 여러분 앞에 있는 것은 40년 전에 만들어진 용감한 사자라는 모형 비행기이고, 이 작은 비행기는 Peter Strokes가 디자인했습니다. 이 비행기는 날개 폭이 비교적 작고, 200갤런의 연료 용량, 그리고 5명의 승객을 위한 좌석을 가지고 있습니다.

Question 2

This Sunday, →/ the staff members →/ of The Aussie Grill →/ will invite →/ you and your family →/ to our restaurant. ↘// We open →/ twenty-four hours a day, →/ and breakfast, ↗/ lunch, ↗/ and dinner →/ are always available. ↘// If you arrive before noon, →/ don't forget to ask →/ a staff member →/ for free drinks. ↘//

이번 주 일요일, The Aussie Grill의 직원들이 여러분과 여러분의 가족을 저희 레스토랑에 초대할 것입니다. 저희는 24시간 영업하며, 아침, 점심, 저녁 식사는 항상 가능합니다. 정오 전에 오시면, 직원에게 무료 음료를 요청하는 것을 잊지 마세요.

Question 3

장소	This picture was taken at an outdoor cafe.	이 사진은 카페 야외에서 찍힌 사진입니다.
인원	Three people are sitting around the table.	세 사람이 테이블에 둘러앉아 있습니다.
중심 대상	On the right, a man is browsing the Internet on his laptop. In the center, a woman is watching his computer while smiling. On the left, a man is drinking coffee.	오른쪽에 있는 한 남자는 그의 노트북으로 인터넷 서핑을 하고 있습니다. 가운데에는 한 여성이 웃으며 그의 컴퓨터를 보고 있습니다. 왼쪽에 있는 남자는 커피를 마시고 있습니다.
주변 대상	In the background, I can see two more people.	뒤에 두 사람이 더 보입니다.
상황	Overall, it seems they are having a meeting.	전반적으로 그들은 회의를 하는 것 같습니다.

Question 4

| 장소 | This picture was taken on the street. | 이 사진은 거리에서 찍힌 사진입니다. |

| 인원 | Three people are crossing the street. | 세 사람이 길을 건너고 있습니다. |

| 중심 대상 | Two of them are walking at the front, and the other person is following. Behind them, a red bus is running. | 그들 중 두 명은 앞에서 걷고 있고, 다른 한 명은 따라오고 있습니다. 그들 뒤에는 빨간 버스가 지나가고 있습니다. |

| 주변 대상 | On both sides of the street, there are trees and cars parked on the road. | 길 양쪽에는 나무가 있고 차가 도로에 주차되어 있습니다. |

| 상황 | Overall, it feels peaceful and calm. | 전반적으로 평화롭고 차분하게 느껴집니다. |

🔊 Imagine a marketing firm is conducting research about streaming services that allow you to watch movies without downloading them first. You have agreed to participate in a telephone interview about it.

한 마케팅 회사가 영화를 다운로드하지 않고 볼 수 있는 스트리밍 서비스에 대해 조사를 하고 있다고 가정해 보십시오. 당신은 이와 관련된 전화 인터뷰에 참여하기로 동의하셨습니다.

Question 5

Q How often do you watch movies, and where do you usually watch them?

당신은 얼마나 자주 영화를 보나요? 그리고 보통 어디에서 영화를 보나요?

A I watch movies once or twice on weekends, and I usually watch them at home.

저는 영화를 주말에 한두 번 보고, 주로 집에서 봅니다.

Question 6

Q Would you be willing to pay for streaming services to watch movies? Why or why not?

당신은 영화를 보기 위해 스트리밍 서비스 사용료를 지불하시겠습니까?
이유는 무엇입니까?

A Definitely. I am actually paying for the Netflix membership because I can watch tons of movies at a low price.

물론입니다. 넷플릭스 회원권을 이용 중인데, 그 이유는 저렴한 가격으로 많은 영화를 볼 수 있기 때문입니다.

Q Which of the following is the most important factor when choosing a movie on a streaming service?

- Viewers' ratings
- Genre
- Reviews written by famous critics

스트리밍 서비스에서 영화를 선택할 때 가장 중요한 요소는 무엇인가요?

- 시청률
- 장르
- 유명한 평론가들이 쓴 비평

IM3-IH I would consider critics' reviews most important, and here is why.

First, their reviews are reliable because <u>they have expertise in analyzing movies</u>.

Second, <u>critics suggest a film that is not worth watching</u>.

This is why.

저는 평론가들의 비평을 가장 중요하게 생각할 것이고, 여기 그 이유가 있습니다.

첫째, 그들의 리뷰는 영화 분석에 대한 전문성이 있기 때문에 신뢰할 수 있습니다.

둘째, 비평가들은 볼 가치가 없는 영화를 제안합니다.

이것이 그 이유입니다.

AL-AH I would consider critics' reviews most important, and here is why.

First, their reviews are reliable because <u>they have expertise in analyzing and evaluating movies</u>. They are trained to examine different aspects of a film, so it's worth considering their opinions.

Second, it's time and money saving. Because <u>critics' recommendations can help me avoid a film that is not worth watching</u>.

This is why.

저는 평론가들의 비평을 가장 중요하게 생각할 것이고, 여기 그 이유가 있습니다.

첫째, 그들의 리뷰는 영화를 분석하고 평가하는 전문성을 가지고 있기 때문에 신뢰할 수 있습니다. 그들은 영화의 다양한 측면을 검토하도록 훈련을 받았기 때문에 그들의 의견을 고려할 가치가 있습니다.

둘째, 시간과 돈이 절약됩니다. 왜냐하면 비평가들의 추천은 제가 볼 가치가 없는 영화를 보지 않도록 도움을 줄 수 있기 때문입니다.

이것이 그 이유입니다.

Yorktown Community Center One-day class
November 2, Symbol community center

Simple baking	10:00 – 11:30 A.M.	Allen Phillip	Room A
Irish dance	2:00 – 3:30 P.M.	Rose Moore	Main Hall
Japanese cooking	3:30 – 4:30 P.M.	Jason Molina	Room C
Zumba dance	4:30 – 5:00 P.M.	Nicole Kimberly	Room A
Introduction of painting	5:00 – 6:30 P.M.	~~Michael Phillip~~ *Changed to Alan Bell*	Main Hall
Drawing	7:00 – 8:30 P.M.	Kevin Stella	Main Hall

🔊 Hi, can I ask a few questions about the one-day class on November 2nd held at the symbol community center?

안녕하세요, 11월 2일 Symbol 주민센터에서 하는 일일 수업에 대해 몇 가지 질문해도 될까요?

Question 8

Q I heard that there will be a 'Simple baking' class. What time will the 'Simple baking' class be, and who is the instructor of the class?

'간단하게 빵 굽기' 수업이 열린다고 들었어요. '간단하게 빵 굽기' 수업은 몇 시이며, 그 수업의 강사는 누구입니까?

A The 'Simple baking' class will be from 10:00 to 11:30 A.M., and its instructor is Allen Phillip.

'간단하게 빵굽기' 수업은 오전 10시부터 11시 30분까지 진행되며, 강사는 Allen Phillip입니다.

Q I was very impressed by the instructor Michael Phillip when taking a one-day class at your center last time. And I heard that Michael Phillip will teach the 'Introduction of painting' course. Could you confirm this information?

저는 일전에 주민센터 일일 수업을 들을 때 Michael Phillip 선생님이 매우 인상 깊었습니다. 그리고 Michael Phillip이 '그림 입문' 수업을 진행한다고 들었어요. 이 정보를 확인해 주시겠습니까?

A Sure, Michael was supposed to teach the 'Introduction of painting' class, but it's been changed to Alan Bell. I am sorry.

물론입니다, Michael이 '그림 입문' 수업을 하기로 되어 있었는데, Alan Bell로 바뀌었습니다. 죄송합니다.

Question 10

Q Could you give me all the details of the dance classes?

댄스 수업에 대한 모든 세부 사항에 대해 알려주시겠어요?

A Sure, there are two. First, we have an 'Irish dance' class from 2:00 to 3:30 P.M. in the Main Hall. And it will be taught by Rose Moore. Second, we have a 'Zumba dance' class from 4:30 to 5:00 P.M. in Room A, and the instructor is Nicole Kimberly. That's all.

물론이죠, 두 개 있습니다. 먼저, 우리는 메인 홀에서 오후 2시부터 3시 30분까지 '아일랜드 댄스' 수업을 합니다. 그리고 이 수업은 Rose Moore가 가르칠 것입니다. 두 번째로, A 룸에서 오후 4시 30분부터 5시까지 '줌바 댄스' 수업이 있으며, 강사는 Nicole Kimberly입니다. 이상입니다.

🔊 Do you agree or disagree with the following statement?
"Employees have more work done when they have flexible schedules."

다음 명제에 동의하십니까, 동의하지 않으십니까?
"직원들은 탄력근무제로 일할 때 더 많은 일을 하게 됩니다."

IM3 I agree that employees have more work done when they have flexible schedules. There are two reasons for this.

First, it's pliable. For example, the employees can work and rest whenever they want. So, it's productive and effective.

Second, it's convenient and comfortable. For instance, they will work more efficiently because they have more freedom.

These are the reasons why I think in this way.

저는 직원들이 탄력근무제로 일할 때 더 많은 일을 한다는 것에 동의합니다. 여기에는 두 가지 이유가 있습니다.

첫째, 유연합니다. 예를 들어, 직원들은 그들이 원할 때 언제든지 일하고 쉴 수 있습니다. 그래서 생산적이고 효과적입니다.

둘째, 편리하고 편안합니다. 예를 들어, 그들은 자유롭기 때문에 더 효율적으로 일할 것입니다.

이것들이 제가 이렇게 생각하는 이유입니다.

IH I agree that employees have more work done when they have flexible schedules. There are two reasons for this.

First, it's pliable. For example, <u>the employees can work and rest whenever they want</u>. So, it's productive and effective. Flexible work schedules will give them a more comfortable working environment.

Second, it's convenient and comfortable. For instance, <u>they will work more efficiently</u> without pressure and tension because they have more freedom.

These are the reasons why I think in this way.

저는 직원들이 탄력근무제로 일할 때 더 많은 일을 한다는 것에 동의합니다. 여기에는 두 가지 이유가 있습니다.

첫째, 유연합니다. 예를 들어, 직원들은 그들이 원할 때 언제든지 일하고 쉴 수 있습니다. 그래서 생산적이고 효과적입니다. 유연한 업무 일정은 그들에게 더 편안한 근무 환경을 제공할 것입니다.

둘째, 편리하고 편안합니다. 예를 들어, 그들은 더 자유롭기 때문에 압박과 긴장 없이 더 효율적으로 일할 것입니다.

이것들이 제가 이렇게 생각하는 이유입니다.

AL-AH I agree that employees have more work done when they have flexible schedules. There are two reasons for this.

First, it's pliable. For example, <u>the employees can work and rest whenever they want</u>. So, it's productive and effective. Since everyone has different routines and work habits, flexible work schedules will give them a more comfortable working environment.

Second, it's convenient and comfortable. For instance, <u>they will work more efficiently</u> without pressure and tension because they have more freedom. So, it's worth it.

These are the reasons why I think in this way.

저는 직원들이 탄력근무제로 일할 때 더 많은 일을 한다는 것에 동의합니다. 여기에는 두 가지 이유가 있습니다.

첫째, 유연합니다. 예를 들어, 직원들은 그들이 원할 때 언제든지 일하고 쉴 수 있습니다. 그래서 생산적이고 효과적입니다. 모든 사람들은 다른 일정과 작업 습관을 가지고 있기 때문에, 유연한 업무 일정은 그들에게 더 편안한 작업 환경을 제공할 것입니다.

둘째, 편리하고 편안합니다. 예를 들어, 그들은 더 자유롭기 때문에 압박과 긴장 없이 더 효율적으로 일할 것입니다. 그래서, 탄력근무제는 가치가 있습니다.

이것들이 제가 이렇게 생각하는 이유입니다.

MEMO